CULTURAL DECEPTIONS

How progress is making us miserable
and how we can get back on track

DR ASHLEY HUMPHREY

First published 2025 by:
Australian Academic Press Group Pty. Ltd.
www.ausapress.com

Copyright Ashley Humphrey © 2025.

Copying for educational purposes
The *Australian Copyright Act 1968* (Cwlth) allows a maximum of one chapter or 10% of this book, whichever is the greater, to be reproduced and/or communicated by any educational institution for its educational purposes provided that the educational institution (or the body that administers it) has given a remuneration notice to Copyright Agency (CA) under the Act.
For details of the CA licence for educational institutions contact:
Copyright Agency, Level 12/66 Goulburn Sreet, Sydney, NSW 2000.
E-mail info@copyright.com.au

Production and communication for other purposes
Except as permitted under the Act, for example a fair dealing for the purposes
of study, research, criticism or review, no part of this book may be reproduced,
stored in a retrieval system, or transmitted in any form or by any means electronic,
mechanical, photocopying, recording or otherwise without prior written permission
of the copyright holder.

 A catalogue record for this book is available from the National Library of Australia

ISBN 9781923114104   (paperback)
ISBN 9781923114111   (ebook)

Disclaimer
Every effort has been made in preparing this work to provide information based on accepted standards and practice at the time of publication. The publisher and author, however, make no representations or warranties with respect to the accuracy or completeness of the contents of this book and specifically disclaim any implied warranties of merchantability or fitness for a particular purpose. It is sold on the understanding that the publisher is not engaged in rendering professional services and neither the publisher nor the author shall be liable for damages arising herefrom. If professional advice or other expert assistance is required, the services of a competent professional should be sought.

Publisher & Editor: Stephen May
Cover design: Luke Harris, Working Type Studio
Typesetting: Australian Academic Press
Printing: Lightning Source

'It occurred to him that his scarcely perceptible attempts to struggle against what was considered good by the most highly placed people, those scarcely noticeable impulses which he had immediately suppressed, might have been the real thing, and all the rest false.' — Leo Tolstoy, *The Death of Ivan Ilyich*.

Contents

Acknowledgments vii

About the Author ix

Part 1: Life in the Modern World

Chapter 1: A Brave New World..3

Chapter 2: Cultural Confusions 13

Chapter 3: 'Me' before 'We'..27

Chapter 4: Buying Happiness...41

Chapter 5: Happiness and its Discontents 55

Chapter 6: Reimagining Wellbeing.....................................71

Part 2: Towards Change

Chapter 7: Lessons from a Pandemic 85

Chapter 8: The Examined Life..99

Chapter 9: A Good Life is a Meaningful Life 117

Chapter 10: Concluding Thoughts 131

Endnotes..139

Bibliography 151

Cultural Deceptions: How progress is making us miserable and how we can get back on track

Acknowledgments

This book would not have been possible without the support of a large number of friends and colleagues. Firstly, to Associate Professor Matthew Klugman, who, upon hearing my intentions to write this manuscript over a friendly catch-up, became a key support and guide in the early stages of the writing process. From helping me craft a book proposal, to then voluntarily reading numerous drafts of said proposal, your mentorship and input were critical in transforming this work from an idea and into a reality. Along these lines, I must also thank Debbie Golvan, whose early support and publishing expertise were what took this work from nothing more than a file on my computer to something read by publishers. This work is also heavily indebted to the intellectual input of my former doctoral supervisors, Associate Professor Pascal Molenberghs, Dr Ana-Maria Bliuc, and Associate Professor Roseanne Misajon. Your scholarly mentorship echoes throughout the pages of this book, as does the way in which you helped frame my early research on the topics it explores. I am very thankful to my current colleagues and research collaborators. In particular, I am immensely thankful for the amazing support and guidance I have received from Professor Helen Forbes-Mewett, who has been a wonderful friend, mentor and collaborator in my professional walk. Also to Professor Brock Bastian, whose time and guidance after the completion of my PhD I am so grateful for, and from whom I learnt so much. To Richard Eckersley, whose writings helped inspire a fascination within me in the area of culture and health in the first place, and I am very grateful for the communication we have shared over the years. To both William Power and Michael Webb for their thorough critiques of the manuscript, thank you for your time and very helpful feedback.

To Stephen May and his team at Australian Academic Press, thank you for all your support and guidance in this journey to publication. Lastly, to my wonderful family and friends. Thank you.

About the Author

Ashley Humphrey completed his PhD in Psychology at Monash University, where he continues to work as a researcher and lecturer in the Social Sciences. He is also active in a number of organisations aimed at supporting disengaged young people. Having travelled the world far and wide, he holds a fascination with how differing cultural environments can influence every sphere of a person's life. His written work exploring this has been published in international scientific journals as well as the popular press. He lives in Melbourne, Australia, and this is his first book.

Cultural Deceptions: How progress is making us miserable and how we can get back on track

Part 1

Life in the Modern World

Cultural Deceptions: How progress is making us miserable and how we can get back on track

Chapter 1

A Brave New World

In the early 1930s, amidst a context of dramatic social change and political instability across the globe, British novelist Aldous Huxley published one of the most significant novels of the twentieth century: *A Brave New World*. Here, Huxley tells the story of a dystopian future world that follows the mantra: 'Everybody's happy nowadays'. Pain, emotional suffering and physical illness have been overcome, and instead people live lives unbound by the 'imperfections' of societies past. Written as a critique of the advances in science and technology that were evolving at the time, Huxley masterfully describes the severe costs of pursuing this ideal utopia. Whilst citizens are engineered both scientifically and socially to live in a highly ordered society with no unemployment nor crime, they are also subjected to a range of prohibitions deemed necessary by their dictatorship to foster this perfect and painless society. These include the condemnation of close social relationships between citizens — as 'everyone belongs to everyone else', outlawing falling in love in favour of strictly casual encounters, and banning the reading of religious and philosophical texts. Happiness is instead sourced from the consumption of materialistic items, sports, and the pleasure-inducing drug 'soma'.

Much like the backdrop to Huxley's imagined future society, the previous few decades have seen dramatic technological, economic, and social changes across the developed world, with its rapid and endless pursuit of a 'Brave New World'. Within the timeframe of a single generation, the internet has revolutionised how people communicate, while also providing us with information on demand. Modern industrialisation and corporate capitalism have enabled greater economic freedom for more people than ever before, allowing the average person living in Western Europe today to be incomparably wealthier than their early twentieth-century ancestors. Advances in medicine and health care have seen the average British life expectancy increase by an entire decade from 1970 to today. And, despite persistent threats of terror as well as ongoing conflicts across the globe, people living in politically stable and economically secure countries are today broadly speaking markedly less likely to die from acts of combat or physical violence than those living in such contexts only a few centuries ago.[1]

Given these progressions, one could reasonably assume that those living in developed, peacetime environments today experience better wellbeing and life satisfaction when compared with previous generations. That's not to say that quality of life in these contexts is universally improved, with health outcomes still shaped by modern civilisation's hierarchies, including class, gender, race, and income level. Further, global challenges broadly consistent with those faced throughout human history, such as war, political unrest, economic pressures, environmental concerns and pandemics, continue to affect the lives of everyday people today. Despite the persistence of such challenges, some statistical evidence points toward improving health outcomes and a higher quality of life for those living in high-income nations across recent decades. Universally, figures from such countries show a steady increase in life expectancy and physical health indicators over the past fifty years, with further data indicating increases in people's average incomes, levels of education and overall living standards across this time span.[2]

Specific to the United States, people are today shown to attain higher levels of education and enjoy better material living standards compared to past generations.[3] At the same time, 85% of Australians report experiencing 'good or very good' health, a result aligning with broader trends indicating improvements in quality of life across a range of measures.[4] Similar findings of increasing quality of life and health indicators have also been reported in New Zealand, Canada and Ireland, and across Western European countries, including Belgium, Germany and the Netherlands.[5]

With significant advancements in medical care, technology and broader access to education and employment opportunities, the steady improvement of the health and quality of life of people living in developed, politically stable and conflict-free societies is well documented. And yet, despite these reported developments, there also seems to be a counter-narrative to such progress. One specific to people's psychological wellbeing. This narrative is expressed in a variety of ways, be it through popular press outlets, within scientific and political discourse, and perhaps most visibly by way of celebrities publicly declaring their mental health battles. It is increasingly scientific (as we will see later in this chapter) but remains largely anecdotal, and it seems to go against the trend of improving benchmarks for people's wellbeing across the modern world. As Australian Scientist Richard Eckersley points out, the discourse around life in the modern world often disproportionately focuses on the positive aspects of life in these contexts and fails to capture key aspects around life stressors and psychological health concerns.[6] Blinded by the improvements in economic and physical health outcomes across the developed world, researchers and the public alike have often ignored the mounting evidence that paints a bleaker picture of life within these societies.

Whilst physical health and quality of life indicators are shown to have improved from previous generations to now, other metrics suggest the mental health of people living in high-income countries is in decline. Reviews of mental health statistics in developed countries across previous generations have shown increasing rates of depression, anxiety and substance use disorders over recent decades.[7] Whilst the authors of these studies note several complicating factors relevant to this increase, including the influence of population growth and increasing life expectancies, they unanimously suggest that these findings require greater attention, outlining the significant burden these increases are having on both health systems and societies alike.

You may or may not see these findings as alarming. And if you possess scepticism around the declining state of mental health across the developed world today versus yesteryear, you have every right to. There are indeed a range of rebuttals to this idea. For instance, one of the first challenges that arises when comparing statistics on mental health from one generation to another is the increasing prevalence today in the diagnosis of psychological illnesses (inclusive of depression and anxiety) compared to previous generations. This increase is in no small part due to the awareness we today have of mental health issues, their symptoms, and their significance in hindering every aspect of a person's life. Today, it is much more likely, for example, that a young person living in the UK from a middle to upper-class background would seek out some sort of professional help if they were experiencing symptoms of depression (thus securing a diagnosis). This would not have been as clear-cut 20–30 years ago when an understanding of depressive symptoms and access to psychological help was far more limited. More generally speaking, the 'just get on with it' mentality often prevailed.

Other sceptics say that findings of increasing mental distress today are a product of changing research interests rather than growing unhappiness. These critics note that there has been a significant shift over the past few decades in defining what symptomology exists as ill-psychological health.[8] Focusing on depression as an example of this, American Sociologist Alan Horitz shares that before the 1970s, this was understood as a 'relatively rare condition', which involved 'feelings of intense meaninglessness and worthlessness', which could lead to suicidal tendencies.[9] Today, classifications of depression are more inclusive. As a result of this greater inclusivity, as Horwitz continues, the feelings of discouragement and disappointment one may experience following the loss of their job or a relationship breakdown — feelings that once would have been perceived as a natural reaction to an adverse life experience — may by today's metrics still come to be categorised today as symptoms of depression. This change in how we define mental health disorders is demonstrated by the increasing list of psychological illnesses outlined in the Diagnostic and Statistical Manual (DSM) of the American Psychiatric Association, which has more than tripled over the past fifty years.

As a consequence of these changing interpretations and semantics around mental illness, comparing mental health statistics of today versus yesteryear is fraught with difficulty, leaving us with a resultant subjectivity and overall lack of clarity in how mental health figures compare from one generation to the next. There are some important exceptions to this, however, in research studies that have used identical measures for symptoms of anxiety and depression at different time points to more accurately compare mental health statistics across differing generations.[10] Research studies that have adopted this approach have been conducted on different generations of young people in countries including the US, the UK, and the Netherlands. Findings from these studies unanimously show an increase in the frequency in which people reported symptoms of anxiety and depression over the previous few decades, providing support to the view that psychological problems have, in fact, increased across the developed world over recent decades.

Regardless of how you interpret current trends in mental health, as many wellbeing scholars have pointed out, it does not mean that the prevalence of these issues today is nothing to be concerned about. At a bureaucratic level, this is well understood, with a recent report from the World Health Organization (WHO) labelling depression as one of the most significant burdens of disease faced by those living in middle and upper-income countries today.[11] Their data shows that as of the year 2021, more than 280 million people worldwide suffer from depression. WHO categorises symptoms of depression as distinct from normal mood fluctuations and emotional responses by their enduring and debilitating nature. In extreme cases, they identify that depressive symptoms can manifest in suicide, which is alarmingly one of the leading causes of death for 15–29-year-olds living in the developed world today. Despite an increasing number of pharmaceutical and therapeutic treatments now available for depression, World Health Organization data shows that depression trends are, in fact, rising. Their figures suggest a steady increase in the number of people suffering from depression over recent decades. They also show high-income countries, including Australia, the US and Finland, to have amongst the highest instances of people affected per population, while island nations Papua New Guinea, Timor-Leste and the Philippines are shown to have amongst the least.[12]

Interestingly, it was only a few decades ago that WHO declared obesity among the most significant health issues faced by the Western world. This 'epidemic', as it was labelled, occurred amidst the backdrop of a highly evolved knowledge regarding good nutrition, the importance of exercise and advances in food engineering designed to promote healthier diets. And yet, the Western environments had cultivated a culture of fast food and increasingly sedentary lifestyles, which was causing more and more people to be unhealthily overweight. Much like this obesity epidemic that emerged across the developed Western world in the 1990s, it seems conceivable that despite all the social, economic and health-related advancements we have made over the previous few decades, we are in the midst of a 'mental health epidemic' — an epidemic that is perhaps also heavily contributed to by the culture we have cultivated across the Western world today.

Research led by American psychologist and pioneer in the field of culture and mental health Jean Twenge, reinforces this idea. Across several research studies, Twenge and her colleagues evaluated young Americans' annual responses to a range of surveys measuring their personality traits, life goals, social practices and mental health collected over the past fifty years.[13] Their analysis indicated firstly a substantial increase in the psychological health issues experienced by young

Americans across the past few decades. Interestingly, corresponding with this rise in mental health issues, the researchers also identified substantial 'generational shifts' in American people's life goals, personal values and social practices over this period. Their results, for example, showed that the millennial generation (those born between 1983 and 1996) are less caring towards others than previous generations and more focused on self-serving and materialistic aims.[14] Linking these collective shifts back to the proposed diminishing mental health of American young people, Twenge and her co-authors suggest these generational changes to people's social values and life ambitions are likely relevant contributors to this decline.

These findings provide an interesting perspective on the possible effect cultural influences may be having on people's mental health. Could it possibly be that, despite all the economic, technological and health-related advancements accompanying modern life, we have created a culture in which psychological wellbeing and life satisfaction have actually declined? Could it be that much like Huxley's dystopian future London, there have been some severe consequences in our pursuit of creating the best of all possible worlds? To be sure, not everyone takes 'soma' to ease their peace of mind, and monogamous relationships are certainly not against the law. But have capitalism's allures of material riches led us away from behaviours and values that best foster our psychological health? Have the many social freedoms afforded to us today encouraged us to be less socially active and made us more withdrawn and isolated than ever before? And has the secularisation of our culture, along with a heightened disinterest in philosophical discourse, left us impervious and apathetic towards the modern pursuit of a meaningful life?

In light of these questions, it is the goal of this book to present evidence that may allow for a more profound critique and understanding of modern society and explore how the prevailing culture can adversely influence individuals' — and societies' — wellbeing and mental health. As a social psychologist, these questions have plagued my mind since my early 20s. It was at this time that I had a close friend confide in me about their experiences of suffering from depression, as well as a complete discontentment with their life. This was a confronting revelation from a friend with whom I had been very close since our early school days. It was particularly striking coming from someone I had always looked up to as a guy who 'had it all together'. This friend came from a seemingly happy family, had solid prospects for the future, and for whom, on the surface, all seemed to be going particularly well. And yet it wasn't. As far as he disclosed, there was no specific catalytic event that led to these symptoms (such as the death of a loved one or a relationship breakdown). His symptoms instead seemed to be related to socially based factors, such as feelings of isolation and loneliness, thoughts of being directionless, and perhaps most significantly, feelings of not 'measuring up' to those around him. Over the years that followed this initial conversation, several other close friends also opened up to me about their experiences of suffering from depression. Again, these were primarily friends who, from the outside, seemed to have everything going for them, possessed suitable social support structures and for whom the future was bright. Their struggles seemed to touch on similar themes to those raised in the initial conversation I had shared with my friend. These other friends also talked about feeling aimless, falling short of certain societal benchmarks, and perpetual dissatisfaction with life.

The earlier mentioned global figures on mental health suggest that my friends are far from alone in their suffering. And in response to the millions of other such cases across the globe, mental health has become a frontline concern for the public health sector the world over. In the UK, 12 billion British taxpayer pounds were poured into the mental health sector in the 2021/22 financial year alone, with this sum being around 10 per cent of the total expenditure by the Department of Health and Social Care. A similar annual percentage of expenditure is allocated to mental health across other high-income countries, including Sweden, Germany and Australia. This money was funnelled mainly into allowing for greater accessibility of psychologists, as well as supporting research into mental health. This is a wonderful thing, with both clinical approaches and further research essential to stemming the increasing tide of mental health challenges experienced by people today. But what if there was a broader societal-based approach that could also assist with the alleviating of this mental health epidemic?

A range of public-level measures were undertaken to address the obesity epidemic of the 1990s and beyond. Community fitness groups were formed, education programs were implemented in schools around the importance of maintaining a healthy diet and routine exercise, and healthier food options emerged in restaurants (even McDonalds!). Most importantly, it was the basic understanding that a lifestyle of overeating unhealthy food and not doing enough exercise was very problematic for one's health that had the most significant effect in curbing the trend towards obesity. Such an understanding may encourage a person to choose a bottle of water over a soft drink to quench their thirst despite the alluring and refreshing nature of the latter. It might instil a desire to walk to work instead of commuting via sitting down in a car or on a bus, even though this may have been the more comfortable option. Ultimately, this understanding has led to people living healthier lives simply by tackling the issue of obesity at the root of its cause.

If culture is in part to blame for the increasing psychological health issues many societies are faced with today, then could not similar societal-level interventions be implemented that disrupt the trend at its origins? This book contends that this could be the case. Through a critique of modern culture, the following pages aim to discuss some of the subtle but critical side effects life in today's world can have on psychological health. In doing so, I hope this book will help you, the reader, engage more critically with the messages and ideals of modern life and perhaps make changes in your own life that will counter these messages in the pursuit of greater personal wellbeing and quality of life.

Chapter 2

Cultural Confusions

> 'The Beauty of the world lies in the diversity of its people'.
> Unknown

When Captain James Cook and his British expedition made their second landing at the Hawaiian Islands in January of 1779, a collision between British and Polynesian cultures ensued. After anchoring nearby Kealakekua Bay, Cook and his fleet chartered to shore to trade with locals and replenish their supplies. The Hawaiian natives were initially highly welcoming and hospitable towards Cook and his crew, so much so that the British are said to have believed the Hawaiians saw them as 'Gods'.[1] This would be one of the first cultural misunderstandings of their stay, with the Hawaiians instead understood to have welcomed the British in accordance with the customs of the Makahiki festive season. This was an annual celebration which took place at this time of year in honour of the God Lono, the Hawaiian God for fertility. As Hawaiian historian Herb Kane writes of this exchange, 'differences of world view and logic between the two cultures often made actions which were perfectly rational to one group seem bizarre or incomprehensible to the other'.[2]

After remaining on the island for just shy of three weeks, Cook and his team set sail, only to return a short while later after intense winds had damaged the main mast of one of their two ships. With the Makahiki season now having concluded, this subsequent encounter saw the British greeted with a far more hostile reception from the Islanders, who perhaps felt the British were now overstaying their welcome. With this tense atmosphere present, a series of further cultural misunderstandings ensued, with fatal results. After accusing the Hawaiians of stealing one of their launch boats, Cook and his team kidnapped the Ali'I Nui (King) of the Island in a bizarre move of retaliation. Suffice it to say this did not go down well. An ugly confrontation between the Hawaiians and the British followed, resulting in a number of casualties including Cook himself. Shortly after Cook's death, an amnesty period was instilled as the British hastily retreated from the island. As they did so, it is said that they were asked by the Hawaiians when Cook would return to seek revenge for his murder. As Kane writes, this was a question rooted in the ancient Hawaiian belief that spirits of the dead may return with 'powers of retribution', and undoubtedly would have provided a challenging message for the British to decipher. To restate Kane's earlier writings: 'actions which were perfectly rational to one group, seem bizarre or incomprehensible to the other'.

Culture Matters

By exploring this early exchange between the British and Polynesian people of Hawaii, we are provided with a vital insight into the importance of cultural customs in determining how humans think, interact and behave. This brief historical narrative depicts these cultural distinctions as influential factors in shaping both parties' behaviours, communication methods and social etiquette. Broadly speaking, culture, as defined by the Cambridge Dictionary, is a phenomenon that is formed around the 'general customs and beliefs of a particular group of people at a particular time'. Philosopher Terry Eagleton writes that culture can relate to 'a whole way of life'. Highly relevant to this exchange between the British and native Hawaiians, culture, Eagleton adds, can be understood as: 'the values, customs, beliefs and symbolic practices by which men and women live'.[3]

Today, we largely distinguish between cultures by applying the broad spectrums of Eastern and Western cultures. Eastern cultures are typically understood to include countries located across Asia as well as the Middle East and are typically categorised by collectivist social values, as well as the influence of the region's major religions, including Islam, Buddhism, Taoism and Hinduism. Tracing its roots back to early European civilisation, Western culture is today a label widely used to refer to traditions of Christian belief systems, as well as a sect of social and political norms that originate from Western Europe. Since its origins, these cultural foundations have been synonymous with a range of economic and political developments that have often been presented as benchmarks of social progress (or at least Western governments like to tell us so). Today, Western culture is conceptualised in several ways, with some of its defining characteristics including democratic political systems, capitalist economies, and individualistic social values.

These are characteristics that are largely consistent with universal definitions of human development. It is therefore no surprise that the overall wellbeing of people living within environments that harness these qualities is shown to be higher when compared with those living in environments that don't. This comparison has been quantified by a wealth of social and medical research that has focused on comparing health outcomes in democratic and economically developed countries versus non-democratic and lower-income countries. These explorations have generally (although not exclusively) shown that those living in wealthier democracies experience better overall health outcomes when compared with those living in lower-income and undemocratic nations.

The late Ed Diener, former Emeritus Professor of Psychology at the University of Illinois, is responsible for decades worth of this investigation into how different cultural variables relate to the wellbeing of a society. By analysing data on different countries' levels of wealth, fundamental values, social preferences, and wellbeing, Diener's synthesised research findings provide the understanding that higher rates of social autonomy, human rights, individualism and ample wealth consistently relate to an increase in the wellbeing of a nation when compared to environments that score lower in these areas.[4] These findings allow us to pinpoint some of the key pillars associated with a flourishing society and subsequently give insight into what specific aspects of a nation's culture best allow its people to universally thrive.

Again, it makes perfect sense that greater levels of freedom and economic wealth would associate positively with a society's wellbeing when compared across cultures. However, for all the indisputable benefits brought about by these qualities, there is curious evidence that suggests they may also carry with them some hidden by-products that can, in turn, be subtly harmful towards a society's psychological health. For example, the many social and economic freedoms that exist across the developed world today compared to days gone past provide people with the enhanced freedom to shape their lives in many different ways, to freely pursue their own personal goals, and to construct their social environment however they may like. Such a level of social freedom exists as a tremendous progress when compared to the forced cooperation to the monarchial or religious-based ruling structures that reigned across most of the world for centuries (and continue to do so in parts of the world today). However, some social critics have also argued that whilst this social autonomy and the many personal freedoms that come with it have allowed for greater independence in people's lives, they have also led to people becoming overly reliant on themselves, less likely to engage with their communities, and consequently more socially disengaged than ever before.[5] Similarly, the economic advantages bought about by the strong capitalist economies present across the developed world, have allowed unparalleled financial freedoms to greater numbers of people than ever before, and in turn have provided for an unquestionable increase in people's quality of life. And yet these economic advances and the social environment they have created have also led to a significant increase in people's level of consumption, debt and materialistic ways of thinking and behaving.

The highly capitalist and individualistic nature of Western society has today fostered a culture whereby aspirations based on personal gain as well as self-focused behaviours are highly normalised. Accordingly, Richard Eckersley suggests that values centred on materialism and self-reliance have become so pronounced across such settings they are now deeply ingrained into prevailing interpretations and definitions of what a good life looks like within these environments. In his book critiquing the economic, health and scientific practices of modern life titled *Well and Good*, Eckersley notes that the 'good life', as it is presented in modern Western settings, acts as a 'Trojan horse' for the promotion of particular values, choices and ambitions in people's lives'.[6] Unlike the Trojan horse used by the ancient Greeks, the propagation of these ideals were never meant to be deceptively harmful to people. Rather, these values and behaviours exist as a cultural by-product of the many aforementioned aspects of the progress we are fortunate enough to live amongst today. The inadvertent consequences of this however, are that many people have misguidedly come to draw on these messages to define and govern their major life goals, values and behaviours. At the extreme end, the idealised life as it is understood in Western contexts today, could be defined by enjoying a career that yields a good level of income and social status, achieving financial security, maintaining a desirable lifestyle, all wrapped up in feelings of boundless and unrelenting happiness. It should be noted here that none of these ideals are problematic in and of themselves. Most of these outcomes are, on the surface, valid and reasonable things to aspire to. Yet, when we place an overstated importance on these desires, and they are pursued at the cost of those shown to be more connected to our deeper psychological needs, they can become problematic. As American Psychologists Edward Deci and Richard Ryan propose, pursuing extrinsically motivated goals, such as material wealth or personal recognition, can overshadow our intrinsic-based needs, such as our innate need to be connected with others.[7] With extrinsic-based behaviours and ambitions tending to centre around the recognition of those around us, Deci and Ryan also note that they can begin to challenge our sense of self-autonomy. They argue that when our behaviours or desires begin to be driven by external rewards and not by our own motives and desires, we can come to 'feel controlled by the rewards' and subsequently bind ourselves to outcomes that may not have any deeper meaning to us. To this end, eminent Polish social theorist Zygmunt Bauman writes that within materialistic societies, earning the money required to keep up with the demands of a consumeristic society as well as the lifestyle it fosters, takes a lot of 'time and energy'. This is energy, Bauman states, that can rob us of the time spent doing the things that truly make us happy: 'It may easily happen, and frequently does, that the losses exceed the gains and the capacity of increased income to generate happiness is overtaken by the unhappiness caused by a shrinking access to the goods which' money can't buy'.[8]

Greater wealth, greater health… right?

It is indeed true that our cultural environment plays a key role in influencing the worldview we come to uphold and, consequently, our interpretation and definition of what makes for a good and meaningful life. With our values and behaviours shaped by what we see happening around us, it makes sense that so many people living in Westernised environments would today affiliate happiness with economic prosperity. After all, progress and stability within such contexts are primarily measured at the political level by economic factors, namely levels of GDP (Gross Domestic Product). Although the initial intentions of measuring GDP never intended its use to extend to gauging social welfare and health-related outcomes, in the absence of more appropriate measurement tools, many have come to use GDP as a key metric for quantifying a society's quality of life. On the surface, this makes a good deal of sense, with higher levels of national wealth allowing for, amongst other things, better medical, education and employment opportunities for a country's population.

Research however has challenged the efficacy of this approach. Recently, a study led by a group of economists from the London School of Economics for instance, explores some of the consequences associated with governments overly relying on using GDP as a measure of progress and quality of life.[9] Here, the researchers suggest that when it comes to a society's quality of life, while a basic economic outcome that allows for adequate living standards is important, the most significant predictors of life satisfaction include good mental and physical health, adequate security and maintaining satisfying relationships with others. These findings led the authors to the conclusion that governments need to shift away from 'proxy measures' of progress, such as gross domestic product and personal income levels, and instead move towards national measures of progress that encapsulate a more universal picture of quality of life.

Such criticisms of using economic measurements as a yardstick of a nation's progress and overall quality of life are not new. Critiquing this approach, Zygmund Bauman writes that: 'pretending that the volume and depth of human happiness can be taken care of and properly served by fixing attention on just one laden GNP — is grossly misleading'.[10] Bauman continues, concluding that the growth of 'national product' is a rather poor measure of the growth of happiness. To illustrate this point further, he uses the example of a now-famous campaign speech given in 1968 by US presidential candidate Robert Kennedy. Here, Kennedy spoke skeptically of this tool, which was becoming a benchmark used to represent all facets of a nation's performance and, in turn, its people's quality of life. Kennedy suggested that GDP measures everything in short, except that which makes life worthwhile'.[11] To justify this point, he listed the many problematic factors that contributed to GDP calculations, such as factories that cause large amounts of air pollution, cigarette advertising, the making of nuclear weapons and the destruction of significant forests. He added that such calculations also fail to take into account metrics reflecting health and education-related factors, the strength of families, or the integrity of government workers and politicians. 'Too much and for too long, we seemed to have surrendered personal excellence and community values in the mere accumulation of material things,' he concluded.

As Bauman notes, it was only months after delivering this speech that Kennedy was dramatically shot in Los Angeles. We can consequently only theorise whether our approach to progress today may have been different had he lived to be elected president of the United States. His criticisms of using GDP as a measurement tool of quality of life encourage us today to look beyond economic barometers for a society's success. Over half a century since Kennedy's address, there has been substantial evidence that the developed world has passed a threshold, a point beyond which economic growth (as it's currently defined) ceases to improve quality of life. As Richard Eckersley states: 'New indicators that adjust GDP for social and environmental factors suggest the trends in GDP and national wellbeing, once moving together, are now diverging'.[12] Might it be that this economic-focused means of measuring progress in the West has for too long overshadowed a dramatic decline in the overall quality of life and psychological wellbeing of its citizens?

Seeking to explore this question, some research colleagues and I conducted a series of interviews with young Australians in order to gauge how this environment fixated on all things economic may be influencing their values, aspirations and mental health.[13] To do this, we asked participants a series of questions about their goals for the future, how they would define success and happiness in the context of their own lives, as well as how they were faring with their psychological health. Of those interviewed, a considerable majority spoke of financial and materialistic based factors as being highly embedded within their conceptualisations of happiness and what a good life looked like to them. Outcomes such as earning a significant income, achieving recognition in their careers, and being able to afford the lifestyle they desired were frequent responses to how participants saw their attainment of happiness in the future. On the other hand, aspirations centred on maintaining strong social relationships with others, personal growth and working towards the betterment of society were seldom brought up. Interestingly, when asked questions about the causes of any worry and stress in their lives, participants also listed factors related to these lifestyle aspirations they held, including how their current achievements compare with those of other people their age, pressures to maintain their image, as well as poor social support as some of the key contributors to the stressors and anxieties they were experiencing. These responses draw a parallel with research conducted in the US led by Sociologist Christian Smith, whose interviews with a large number of young Americans similarly showed that the aspirations young people had for their futures were largely 'self-serving' and 'materialistic' in nature.[14] These aims included acquiring a financially rewarding career, pursuing their desired lifestyle, as well as achieving material prosperity. As with our Australian interviewees, very few of the US young people interviewed responded with desires to change the world, lead healthy and fulfilling lives, or become leaders within their communities. These are troubling findings, and yet, as Smith and his team note, it should come as no surprise that the current generation of young people would feel this way. When growing up in a Western environment today, people's lives from their earliest school days are programmed towards the objectives of achievement, with the idealised end goal of attaining a financially stable career. Yet throughout this process, very little attention is nowadays paid to developing a person's whole self, inclusive of their unique traits and abilities, as well as their values and sense of personal identity. Add in the competition of a globalised job market, rising living costs, as well as a generation of people who live large parts of their lives externally through social media, and you see a social climate that would naturally lead people to uphold such beliefs about what's most important for their lives and futures.

Such pressures contribute heavily to how we conceptualise the 'good life' in Western contexts, as well as the subsequent values and aspirations people in these environments come to pursue. And yet, this approach to life is a long way removed from traditional religious and philosophical ideas around what makes for a flourishing existence. Within his *Apology* text, Plato draws on a phrase spoken by his mentor Socrates to define what he sees as the key tenets of the quintessential good life. Spoken right before his execution for teaching 'radical ideas', Socrates responded to his choice of death over a commitment to stop his teachings by stating that 'unexamined life is not worth living'.[15] This statement exists today as perhaps the most recited piece of Western philosophical wisdom in history. Plato unpacks Socrates' statement by suggesting that the 'good life' revolves around doing what we can to use our passions to strive towards a purpose that builds up our community and transcends our selves. Plato remarks that aspirations and values are important not just for a functioning society but also for the wellbeing of the individual. These ideas match many traditional faith-based ideas around life's most important facets, which often emphasise love, relationships and community affiliation as essential for optimal human functionality and contentment. Psychological needs theories would further support these ideas, citing elements such as our social relationships, personal growth and acts of kindness towards others as key contributors to our happiness and psychological wellbeing. And yet this version of 'the good life' as we have come to define it in a Western context, seems to revolve more than ever before around self-serving, hedonistic and materialistic factors, with such a focus overshadowing our innate psychological needs.

It is worth noting here that a range of factors are relevant in determining how much our cultural environment may influence and shape our behaviours and may in turn impact on our health. As any introductory sociology course will teach you, variables such as one's ethnic background, religious beliefs, and age are all important in shaping how we perceive and engage with the cultural customs of the environment that surrounds us. It is also true that within any cultural setting, individuals carry a level of autonomy over their lives and how they choose to live them. It is highly likely, for instance, that an elderly woman who migrated to Sydney after spending the first half of her life living in Ukraine and has remained engaged in the local Ukrainian diaspora community ever since would perceive and interact with the cultural environment that surrounds them very differently, to say a young Sydneysider who has lived in the city their entire life. Despite living in the very same city, these two people would likely lead quite different lives, inclusive of their values, social habits and even fashion choices. And yet, whilst different people might have very divergent experiences of living within the same cultural setting, our surrounding environment is still likely to play a pervasive role in the way we think, behave, and what we aspire to. If you have ever purchased an item of clothing considered to be 'in fashion', for example, it is highly likely that in some way a cultural message drove the decision to make that purchase, whether you were conscious of it or not. In the same way culture may dictate what clothes we choose to wear, it also seems self-evident that cultural characteristics and values can have an equally significant impact on our thought practices and behaviours and in turn, our psychological health. Interestingly, we are often more active in critiquing the various cultural messages we receive regarding the latest clothing fashions than we are in critiquing the messages our society is similarly conveying to us about what's most important for a good life. If we want to improve our psychological health (both personally and societally), it therefore seems crucial we take a more critical approach to the cultural landscape we are confronted with today, as well as the resultant principles that guide our lives that we take from it.

****

Returning to the exchange outlined at the beginning of this chapter between the British explorers and the people of the Hawaiian Islands. It goes without saying that a visit to these islands today would provide a very different experience from that which Captain James Cook and his crew encountered in the late 1700s. Annexed by the United States in the late nineteenth century, Hawaii now exists as the fiftieth state of the US. This is visibly reflected in its cultural and geographic landscape, which today boasts high-rise resorts to accommodate the millions of tourists it welcomes every year, along with American fast-food chains and shopping malls spread across the islands. Yet cultural echoes of the past remain strong, kept alive by ancient traditions and customs that still permeate the lives of modern Hawaiians today, and in doing so, demonstrate the enduring and embedded nature of a people's culture. Tragically, however, there have been elements of this culture that have been lost along the way also, including the overthrow of the Hawaiian monarchy, the endangerment of the Hawaiian language as well as the diminished number of culturally significant festivals that remain celebrated. Despite these, as well as an array of other ghastly injustices and hardships brought about by the colonisation of the Hawaiian Islands, there have been some improvements to the quality of life native Hawaiians experience today. These include improved physical health indicators, access to education, and the benefits of modern infrastructure. While these advances do not overshadow the ongoing challenges faced by Native Hawaiians today, they do reflect broader advantages associated with modern life in an economically secure context.

Indeed, the life we have inherited in the twenty-first century allows unprecedented advantages for greater numbers of people to live a good and fulfilling life comparable to any other time in human history. It therefore has not been the intention of this chapter, nor those that follow it, to promote a state of doom and gloom for life in the modern world. Rather, it is intended to explore how cultural characteristics can be, at times, misleading and deceptive in relation to what makes for a good life and what is most important for our psychological health. It wasn't that long ago that hardships formed out of poverty, injustice and discrimination dominated the lives of people all over the world. Accounts of nineteenth-century life, for instance, universally present us with a bleak picture of existence for most of the world's population. This was typified by mass poverty, religious and political subjugation and vast levels of social class indifference. The effects of these social ills are eloquently described by the English poet William Blake in his verse depicting life in London at this time.[16]

> I wander thro' each charter'd street,
> Near where the charter'd Thames does flow.
> And mark in every face I meet
> Marks of weakness, marks of woe.

Fast forward to life in the twentieth century, and you see the first fifty years of its timeline were occupied by two major World Wars just over twenty years apart, a crippling depression that existed in between these conflicts, and many other social atrocities that were to take place the world over. Whilst littered with further conflicts and social unrest, the second half of this century that followed saw a semblance of relative healing and comparative stability take place across most of the Western world, exemplified by a period of economic growth, greater access to education and health care and rapid developments in technology. Today, we can be grateful for these changes, which have allowed us to enjoy the many benefits and freedoms we often take for granted.

Such recent history reminds us that it is indeed a good time to be alive and that there are many positives associated with living in a secure and economically developed society today. These include economic, health, educational, and employment opportunities that past generations, as well as those living in economically disadvantaged circumstances today, would only dream of. Yet despite these substantial advantages, it is clear from the research reviewed thus far on trends in psychological health that there also remain many challenges to life in these contexts. In the following chapters, we will examine these specific challenges and confusions and look at their contribution to the increasing mental health challenges experienced by people living across the developed world today.

Chapter 3

'Me' before 'we'

> 'It is the individual who is not interested in his fellow man who has the greatest difficulties in life and provides the greatest injury to others. It is from among such individuals that all human failures spring.'
> Alfred Adler

In my mid-twenties, I had the privilege of travelling through Indonesia, where I visited a number of its islands scattered across the Flores and Bali Seas. During my travels, I befriended someone from the Lesser Sunda Islands region, who I will give the alias of Mike. Mike was from a small, remote village situated amidst the highlands of the Sunda Islands. This village was largely self-sufficient, with locals surviving mainly off produce harvested around the village. The only exception to this was the essential items that were brought to the region once every few weeks, when a select few villagers would descend the highlands and travel to one of the larger Indonesian islands to the west. In fact, it was the relative duty of anyone who was travelling to any of the larger islands that surrounded the Lesser Sunda Island region to return with clothing, medications, and toothpaste for fellow villagers. Upon meeting Mike, we quickly came across the revelation that we were the very same age. Despite sharing a birthdate, it became clear as we continued talking that the contrast between the lives we had lived to this point in time was, to me, quite dramatic. I grew up in Melbourne, Australia. A city with a population of around five million people. It was there that I was recently afforded the privilege of completing my university degree and was in the process of pursuing the career that I desired. Mike had grown up in a village on the Lesser Sunda Islands, with a population just over a thousand. He had attended the local secondary school there, and upon finishing his education was then sent off to work in one of his island's main exports, tourism. This was a career essentially thrust upon Mike by his village, as it enabled him to acquire money and resources for his village that it needed to continue to function. And Mike was more than happy to oblige. Yet, as our discussion went deeper, Mike shared with me his true desire was to study politics at university, which at this point in time was way beyond his financial means.

As we gazed over the beautiful greenery that surrounded one of Indonesia's many terraced rice fields in perfect serenity, we discussed the course of our lives, including our families, ambitions for the future, and respective local politics. In doing so, there were struggles and hardships Mike shared that I could not even comprehend. Struggles around basic nutritional needs not being met, the unreliable nature of his village's scarce electricity generators, housing that could not cope with the extreme weather conditions the island was often faced with, and a range of other financial-related adversities. And yet, when we discussed our family lives, for example, my narrative also included certain lacks. These were lacks that are best defined as 'poverties of the West'. Here I shared that I had been raised solely by my mum, with my father living on the other side of the Australian continent for the majority of my upbringing. The concept of a single-parent family was foreign to Mike, and he was very inquisitive about this element of my personal history. As our conversation continued, I came to somewhat envy Mike's closeness with his family, his devotedness to his community and the evident support structures he had in place within his world.

This notion that Mike described, of putting the needs of his community ahead of his own, sounds like an attitude that would be unique to an isolated and resource-challenged setting like the remote village he grew up in. Within an environment such as this, a mutual dependence on one another would seemingly be quite important for the community to function. And yet, cross-cultural research shows us that many Eastern and traditionally collectivistic countries still largely embody social values such as these today. By collectivistic, I mean a social orientation that puts the needs and goals of one's community ahead of their own. This notion is well articulated by Mike's situation, with such values typically thriving in environments whereby mutual cooperation and the support of others is necessary for a community's survival. These ideals differ from 'individualistic' based social values that instead emphasise the freedom of the individual to pursue their own personal goals and form relationships with others in whatever way they may choose. Socially orientating oneself in an individualistic way, therefore, does not preclude one from having an immediate circle of friends, nor having an interest in or even involvement in their community. Instead, it allows the individual to make their own social choices, unbound to the wants or needs of the greater collective.

The Evolution of Western Individualism

Individualistic practices are widely understood to have taken root across the Western world during the time of the Industrial Revolution — a period when vast numbers of people left behind life in rural villages and the communally focused traditions they fostered, in pursuit of work in the increasingly industrialised and capitalist cities of the world. Fast-forward to the twenty-first century and Zygmunt Bauman argues that 'modern society exists in its incessant activity of individualising', adding that individualistic values and beliefs are amongst the defining social characteristics of modern Western cultures.[1]

A range of cross-cultural research validates this proposition, with findings from Dutch social psychologist Geert Hofstede showing that Western countries such as the US, the UK, France and Australia are all highly individualistic in their social preferences.[2] These are environments Hofstede defines as possessing a 'loosely knit' social framework, whereby individuals are expected to take care of only themselves and their immediate families. At the other end of the scale are countries categorised as collectivistic societies. Hofstede's analyses showed these to include the Pacific Island nation of Fiji, most African nations, and a number of Southeast Asian countries, including Thailand, Cambodia, and Indonesia. Hofstede defines these social environments as operating around a tightly joined communal framework, in which people can expect their family or members of a particular community to 'look after them in exchange for unquestioning loyalty'. Hofstede neatly summarises the distinction between these divergent cultural environments by suggesting that a society's position on being either individualistic or collectivistic is reflected in whether people's self-image is defined in terms of 'I' or 'we'.[3]

The freedom to socially orientate oneself in an individualistic way is one of the most significant societal changes to have taken place across the Western world over the previous few centuries. And yet, outside of philosophical and social science literature, individualism is a term most people would seldom contemplate, let alone associate with their psychological health. When viewed through the lens of history, social scientists recognise the individualistic social movement as a cultural shift that contested enforced religious authority, enhanced people's civic rights, and liberated them from the communal obligations inherent in collectivistic societies — ultimately contributing to a significant increase in personal freedom. Analysing data on social values and happiness collected from over fifty different countries in the mid-1990s, Ed Diener, along with his colleagues, quantified some of these advantages present within individualistic societies.[4] Diener and his team's analysis showed that the economic and social freedoms that accompany individualistic cultures led to a positive association between individualistic countries and subjective wellbeing when compared with collectivist cultures. Specifically, they identified that the greater human rights, social equality, and higher incomes that are characteristic of individualistic societies were among the key predictors of wellbeing between nations.

Findings such as these indicate that there are clearly many positives that come with living in an individualistic environment, which could be summarised in the personal freedoms and agency they provide for. Subsequent research however has suggested that there may be more to this story. Comparing rates of youth suicide across different nations, Richard Eckersley and Greg Dear, for instance, found that suicide figures were highest in individualistic countries where there also existed greater social and economic freedoms.[5] Analysing data collected through the World Values Survey as well as the World Health Organisation, they showed that youth suicide rates were higher in cultures that espoused individualistic social values when compared with more community-focused cultures. From this finding, Eckersley and Dear proposed two factors that contribute to increased suicide rates in individualistic societies. First, such societies possibly fail to provide suitable sources of social identity and attachment, and second, they tend to promote unrealistic or inappropriate expectations of individual freedoms and autonomy. In discussing these ideas, Eckersley and Dear refer to the early sociological work of French theorist Emile Durkheim, who, in the late nineteenth century, proposed that suicide was emphatically linked to low social attachment and a failure of society to successfully integrate the individual.[6] In his famous discourse on suicide, Durkheim concluded that the more socially connected one is to the community that surrounds them, the less likely they are to commit suicide.

Durkheim's ideas and theories appear to today be accurately reflected across modern society. It therefore, seems that in spite of all the benefits provided by living in an individualistic environment, there is likely also a range of pitfalls which can also result in people experiencing greater isolation and poorer social support. Writings from cross-cultural psychologist Harry Triandis have improved our understanding of why individualistic environments may bring about such contradictory outcomes. He wrote about the concepts of both individualism and collectivism as having two separate sub-traits.[7] Triandis proposed that there was a side of individualism that values personal freedom, uniqueness and self-sufficiency, which he labelled 'horizontal individualism'. This differs from a further set of traits he distinguished, which he termed 'vertical individualism', whereby self-sufficiency is again valued, but in a more extreme way, so much so that relationships with others come to be of low importance. Embedded within this type of individualism is also a desire by people to 'stand out' from the crowd and separate themselves from others via competition, achievement, and power. Similarly, Triandis divided collectivism into sub-traits of valuing cooperativeness between an individual and their community (horizontal collectivism) and a complete submission and dutifulness to the authorities of one's community (vertical collectivism).

Intrigued by these differing social attitudes and behaviours associated with individualism, as proposed by Triandis, I, along with some research colleagues, set out to test whether they could have different effects on people's psychological health. More broadly, we were interested to see if these traits could distinguish between the positive and negative effects individualism can seem to have on a person's wellbeing. Using Triandis' sub-definitions, we investigated how orientations towards these differing social traits related to participants' responses to a series of questions measuring their depression, anxiety and stress-related symptoms.[8] Across a number of studies drawing on both Australian and US participants, we found that a high attachment to individualistic values related to competitiveness with others and extreme self-sufficiency (vertical individualism) were significantly associated with lower levels of psychological wellbeing, while orientations towards valuing personal freedom, uniqueness and self-reliance (horizontal individualism) had minimal effect in influencing participants wellbeing. It is well established that overly comparing oneself with others can lead to poorer social relationships and diminished psychological health outcomes, so in that sense, these findings are far from unexpected. What is significant however, is the understanding that in spite of all the social freedoms it provides for, the way the individualistic culture as it has come to be cultivated across the Western world today, can foster attitudes and beliefs that can ultimately be harmful to our mental health. These findings match up with the earlier theorising of Harry Triandis, who in proposing these differing sub-traits of individualism, argued that the autonomy present in individualistic societies could fuel these traits of competitiveness by leading people towards turning 'inwardly' and pursuing personal achievement at the cost of relationships. Triandis writes that this over-dependence on one's self may also come to be very isolating, leading to the mindset that we can achieve success and fulfilment in life entirely on our own, and that these pursuits are best pursued independently.[9] Even though such self-reliance may lead to an increase in a person's resilience and sense of independence, it can also leave them without the social support they may need to prosper and in turn more vulnerable to suffering from feelings of isolation and loneliness.

As far back as the mid-nineteenth century, French social theorist Alexis de Tocqueville wrote with both praise and caution towards the 'American individualism' that he observed as taking root across American society at the time. Touring America from his native France, De Tocqueville wrote in his *Democracy in America* dissertation that American individualism emerged with the motive to, in fact, strengthen the community through the various social freedoms it provided for. However, he added the important caveat that it also held the potential to lead one to: 'sever himself from the mass of his fellows and to draw apart with his family and his friends, so that after he has formed a little circle of his own, he willingly leaves society at large to itself'.[10] At the beginning of the twenty-first century, research from Harvard University Political Scientist Robert Putnam showed how accurate De Tocqueville's theories and predictions were to become. Within his aptly titled bestseller *Bowling Alone*, Putnam discusses the ways in which Americans' engagement with others and community involvement declined significantly from the 1970s onwards. 'During the first two-thirds of the century', Putnam writes, 'Americans took a more and more active role in the social and political life of their communities — in churches and union halls, in bowling alleys and club rooms, around committee tables and card tables and dinner tables...then, mysteriously, and more or less simultaneously, we began to do all these things less often'.[11] From this statement, Putnam compares the American social landscape described by De Tocqueville during the nineteenth century with life today. He suggests the individualistic social environment De Tocqueville wrote of was one whereby people upheld personal goals, yet often did so with the betterment of the broader community in mind, and remained highly engaged in community life. In contrast, Putnam describes the US today as operating in a highly individualised way, suffering heavily from weakened social connections between people. 'Weakened social capital', he writes, 'is manifest in the things that have vanished almost unnoticed — neighbourhood parties and get-togethers with friends, the unreflective kindness of strangers, the shared pursuit of the public good rather than the solitary quest for private goods'.[12] He concludes with the evocative sentiment that this decline in community engagement has us 'bowling alone' — his haunting metaphor for a society he sees as increasingly disconnected and isolated from one another.

Lonely amidst a crowd of people

It seems somewhat ironic that in the big population-dense cities that cater for the bulk of the Western world's population, people experience more loneliness than in isolated communities such as a remote Indonesian Village. And yet, if we can reflect for a moment on what it's like to attend a large party of, say 100 guests versus a small social gathering of half a dozen, we can start to get an idea of how this phenomenon works. Much like the experience of attending a large party, whereby we may feel socially overwhelmed and less obliged to socialise with those present than we would in the scenario of a small gathering, big city environments allow for people to 'blend into the fabric' so to speak, and essentially do their own thing without really having to interact with anyone they don't want to. This might suit a person just fine. One may be perfectly happy spending time with just a select group of people, and only when they may feel like it. However, research shows that engaging with our social networks only when we feel we could use a 'social hit' can be very problematic to our overall health. American social neuroscientists John and Stephanie Cacioppo write that much like the feedback mechanisms of hunger and thirst, feelings of loneliness signal a threat to our wellbeing, born out of an inherent need to belong, and provide one another with 'mutual protections and assistance'.[13] They add that feelings of loneliness can lead to increased blood pressure, poorer sleep outcomes and an overall suppression of the immune system. Further exploring the physiological consequences associated with loneliness, American epigeneticist Steve Cole has concluded through a range of genealogy studies that social isolation and loneliness are an even more potent risk factor for one's health than stress in leading to major disease and depression.[14] Discussing the effects of social isolation on health, he states that: 'Our survival and thriving depends on being part of a community. When we fall out of that sense of connection and community, our bodies respond to that as if we were literally threatened'.

Before this more scientific understanding, writers and scholars alike have for centuries recognised the positive relationship between belonging to a community and mental health. In 1624, English poet John Donne penned the now famous verse: 'No man is an island entire of itself; every man, is a piece of the continent, a part of the main'.[15] These sentiments from Donne fit well with the social processes of a collectivistic society, as illustrated by Mike's story at the beginning of this chapter. It is true that collectivist environments tend to produce more stable social relationships, as well as higher levels of social cohesion, cooperation, and obligation towards key social responsibilities and goals. It therefore seems quite reasonable to assume that in contexts such as these, feelings of loneliness and seclusion would be highly foreign. And yet, research has frequently pointed to collectivist societies experiencing lower levels of wellbeing when compared with individualistic ones. One obvious reason for this is that collectivistic values and behaviours tend to prosper in lower socio-economic contexts. As relationship expert and Professor of Marketing at the University of Michigan Aaron Ahuvia notes, it is in environments such as these whereby collectivistic social practices are often more about forced cooperation that is necessary for a disadvantaged society to function than a set of social preferences.[16] So, whilst collectivistic environments support social cohesion, this cohesion is not necessarily based on people voluntarily choosing to highly engage with those around them. Rather, it is about people fulfilling their forced social roles and responsibilities that are required of them for their community to function, rendering such environments far from social utopias.

From a broad cultural perspective, we can see here that there are drawbacks to socially operating both in a highly collectivistic and highly individualistic way. And yet aspects of both these social orientations are important for nurturing good psychological health, such as the high social cohesion that abounds in collectivistic societies and the social freedoms that exist in individualistic societies. Focusing on individualistic societies, it is clear that the freedom and resultant flexibilities people have to construct their own identities and make key life decisions are essential for a flourishing life. However, it seems this freedom has come to be misused and misunderstood, leading to a range of consequences. Most significantly, these consequences have included people coming to undervalue the importance of building broad social networks and engaging with their communities, and subsequently being too engrossed in matters of the self. This has then manifested in people across the Western world experiencing increasing levels of isolation and loneliness, greater anxiety and confusion in people's sense of identity, and, above all, poorer psychological health outcomes.

As sociologists Anthony Elliot and Charles Lemert neatly put it, 'in the kind of society we live in — that of the polished, expensive, globally networked cities of the west, the lures and seductions of individualism reign supreme'.[17] This pull is made particularly strong when we think about the innate sense of competition fostered amongst individuals by globalised job markets and fluctuating economies. In uncertain and competitive environments such as these, the response of putting oneself first can simply seem like a natural reaction to these pressures. A tactic at best of ambition and personal drive and at worst of self-preservation. And yet there are cultural exceptions to this in capitalist and urbanised countries that still foster a focus on collectivistic and community-oriented social practices. South Korea serves as one example of a highly developed capitalist country that, in spite of all the economic development that has taken place in the country over the past few decades, still espouses a strong sense of community and social cohesion amongst its people. Another example exists in one of the wealthiest countries in the world, Norway, which abides by its social philosophy of *Janteloven* (or the 'law of Jante'). This principle, which is commonly applied across other Nordic countries, also outlines a social edict based on all people being equal and that no individual is bigger than the society that surrounds them. According to the law of Jante, one should not boast about individual accomplishments nor be jealous of another's but should go about business there with the betterment of society in mind. With perspectives such as these, it is little wonder that Scandinavian countries are regularly listed as amongst the happiest in the world. These examples indicate that better social cohesion within the competitive capitalist contexts of the West is possible, and that we do not need to resort to individualistic thinking as a refuge from the many challenges modern society can throw our way.

It would seem that in spite of these challenges, those of us who are fortunate enough to live in a culture that values and promotes freedom of the self and that has the economic and political stability to support these ideals, have a choice. We could heedlessly engage with the wants of our own desires, using our social freedom to exclusively pursue our own needs, comforts and ambitions. Alternatively, we could better serve both society as well as ourselves by using these freedoms towards the means De Tocqueville suggested we should nearly 200 years ago. That is, we should work towards aspirations that may benefit ourselves but also positively impact the larger community in some way, and, in the process, reawaken a greater cohesiveness in our social attitudes. As the poet Alexander Pope wrote in *An Essay on Man*, 'True self-love and social love are the same', implying that caring for those around us is a core accomplice to caring for ourselves.[18] By giving time to other people, our communities, and those closest to us, we benefit not only them but also ourselves. With so many of the anxieties and worries we fixate on in our lives focussed on ourselves, such a practice enables us to think beyond our own individual concerns and in turn, lighten whatever psychological burdens we may be carrying — even if for just a period of time.

****

Reflecting back over my conversations with Mike while exploring the islands of Indonesia, I feel resultantly grateful to have grown up in a culture that enabled me immense freedom to make key life decisions, decide who I want to socialise with, and ultimately gifted me the liberty to decide who I want to be as a person. This independence, as well as the provisions that have gone with it, have allowed me to pursue the goals and dreams I have desired across a range of different areas, and I don't take these social freedoms for granted. There are indeed many positives for a person living in an individualistic society, such as the freedom and independence these environments can cater for. However, there is also a case worth making against the individualistic movement as it has come to manifest across some parts of the world today for the role it has played in harming people's connections to their communities, and the overall strength of one's social support networks. Further, traits that are emblematic of an individualistic society seem to have contributed to a culture of self-promotion, competitiveness and social isolation within these environments.

We could learn a lot from the social systems in place in Mike's Village, where family, community and local matters permeate the core values of each citizen. In her book *America the Anxious* American author Ruth Whippman reinforces this notion by stating that happiness is 'other people', asserting that strong social relationships are the strongest predictors of happiness across cultures.[19] From a personal perspective, we can see that if our social behaviours and attitudes become too individualistic, and in the process, we neglect to engage with the broader community of people that surrounds us, not only will the larger community suffer, but we ourselves will suffer. As Aristotle stated some time ago:

> Man is by nature a social animal. Society is something that precedes the individual. Anyone who either cannot lead the common life or is so self-sufficient as not to need to, and therefore does not partake of society, is either a beast or a God.[20]

We humans need community to function. If we as a society are to move forward toward better mental health outcomes, we must find a way to reconnect with this ancient wisdom by engaging more intentionally with the people around us and our communities at large. As the mantra posted on the locker rooms of countless sporting teams around the world correctly states, we are indeed: 'stronger together'.

Chapter 4

Buying Happiness

> 'Poor and content is rich, and rich enough;
> But riches fineless is as poor as winter
> To him that ever fears he shall be poor;
> Good heaven, the souls of all of my tribes defend
> from jealousy!'
>
> Othello, William Shakespeare

In the mid-nineteenth century, the United States print industry was expanding rapidly, with major newspaper publications dramatically increasing right across the country. It was at this time that Philadelphian businessman Volney Palmer set up what is considered one of the world's first advertising agencies. From the early 1840s, Palmer would place advertisements promoting the goods and services of a litany of businesses in over 1,000 newspapers across North America.[1]

Over the following decades, advertising practices would boom, evolving beyond just print mediums and onto the rooftops of large city buildings, shopfront windows and across film and radio mediums. Media Historian Stewart Ewan writes that as advertising practices continued to develop across the early twentieth century, they began to draw on some of the evolving psychological research that had been conducted at the time to help build their campaigns.[2] These campaigns, Ewan notes, would draw on such research in an attempt to enhance the level of prestige and desirability around the particular product they were trying to promote while also subtly pushing a message of the discontent that life would hold without a particular product in a consumer's psyche. Writing on the successes of these campaigns, Ewen argues that some of these advertisements were so pervasive that they went beyond just selling a particular product but also became deeply entrenched into the American consciousness specific to what it means to be American.

Such an impact is indicative of the influence advertising can have on a society's behaviours and values. From the relatively humble beginnings of Palmer's newspaper advertising agency to the sophisticated marketing campaigns we are inundated with today, the advertising movement has forever changed the way people interact with the world around them. Nowadays, modern corporate advertising is so embedded in our psyche it has become part of our everyday vernacular. For example, if one were to describe the event of a professional sporting fixture they had attended to a friend or colleague today, they would likely recount having watched two rival teams playing in a — insert corporation name here — trophy match. This match would have taken place at a stadium not named after its location or style of architectural design, but that of the corporation that put forward the highest bid towards acquiring its naming rights. Correspondingly, every spare inch of space at this stadium, including its playing surface, would reflect this corporation's logo amongst the insignia of many other companies, with no visible space sacred (not even the players' outfits!). For some, and perhaps even many, this is just a part of life in the economically driven modern world, with marketing efforts such as these bearing little influence over one's consumer-based decisions and behaviours. However, the impact this contemporary form of capitalism has on people's subconscious thought and the subsequent values of our society is worth exploring.

The Evolution of a Consumeristic Society

An array of research, for example, contends that the consumeristic environment that surrounds us in the modern world has successfully managed to influence our lives in ways that go beyond just our consumer behaviours but has been pervasive in shaping our values, attitudes towards others and aspirations for the future.[3] In doing so, this environment has propagated a message that happiness, success, and a meaningful life depend upon particular materialistic benchmarks being met.

These promotions of materialistic ideals are not just restricted to clever marketing campaigns and resultant advertisements that permeate our lives daily. It would therefore be unfair to go back and label the humble Philadelphian entrepreneur Volney Palmer as the man responsible for creating this materialistic and consumption-orientated society we find ourselves living within today. It is also worth noting that early theorising by evolutionary and behavioural psychologists suggests that these materialistic motives may be partly inherent and not necessarily unique to twenty-first-century capitalist life. Such theories propose that the pursuit of wealth and higher social status has for centuries motivated people to strive towards personal growth, which in turn has played a fundamental role in driving society forward. Similarly, behavioural theories suggest that the successful attainment of material rewards is an underlying motive for all human behaviour and fundamental to the progression of society.

History would attest to these ideas, indicating that certain groups of people have always had a motive towards greater riches and status. However, economic historians would tell us that prior to the Industrial Revolution of the mid-eighteenth century, the opportunity to pursue wealth across most societies was a reality only possible for a select few.

In pre-industrial European society, for example, class structures were highly regimented between the aristocracy and the peasantry, with the order of hierarchy you were born into essentially dictating the economic outlook you would face for the remainder of your life. It wasn't until around the time of the Industrial Revolution that emerged from the mid-eighteenth century that European society began to transform into the largely capitalist society we see today. Accompanying this change was the establishment of the middle class (or the *petite bourgeoisie* as they were referred to by Marx) and in turn the opportunity for a far greater population of people to achieve a level of relative wealth than ever before.

The continued evolution of capitalist economies has meant that today, across the developed world, fulfilling one's financial aspirations for the future has never before been so in reach. Even amidst tenuous economic times, higher median incomes, greater opportunities for education, and significant technological advancements have enabled a larger portion of people to live lives of relative affluence when compared to past generations. Specific to the financial liberties we enjoy today, Yuval Noah Harari notes in his bestselling book *Sapiens*, the access we have to borrow money today — a loan that may, for example, allow us to start a business, receive an education, or put a deposit down on a home — allows us the freedom to better ourselves in ways not possible in centuries past. He writes that once upon a time, sourcing the required financial loans necessary to make these dreams a reality would have been immensely difficult across all such circumstances, with access to borrowed funds very difficult to come by. This continues to be true in challenged economic environments today, also making it very difficult for people to progress beyond their present economic circumstances. Such a privileged economic environment is not without its own unique challenges. These challenges can be pronounced when we begin to direct these financial credits that we have available to us towards aims that we don't need, such as luxury consumer items we can't really afford, along with other means of instant gratification. That in turn sees us required to work harder than we otherwise would to pay off such debts. It is this misuse of our finances towards purchases we do not need that has led to the consumeristic mindsets that are so prevalent across the developed world and have led many people to direct their lives and aspirations towards these means and away from life's more important aspects.

The Wealth–Happiness Paradox

The underlying assumption with the economic increases and growing levels of personal wealth that have taken place across the developed world over previous generations was that consistent increases in material affluence would lead to consistent increases in people's wellbeing. To a point, this has unquestionably been the case, with increases in both personal and societal wealth allowing for a substantial improvement in the quality of life people have experienced over the past century. In the 1970s, however, economist Richard Easterlin challenged the understanding that people's quality of life would continue to increase as society continued to get wealthier.[4] To do this, Easterlin explored data on US people's life satisfaction and compared this with the national economic growth that had taken place since the conclusion of the Second World War. In what became known as the Easterlin Paradox, his analysis revealed that despite a consistent growth of the American economy over this time span, US people's happiness and life satisfaction had remained almost unaltered. From this finding, the Easterlin Paradox proposes that whilst life satisfaction does rise with average incomes amongst both individuals and within nations, it does so only to the point that certain basic needs are met and that beyond this benchmark, increases in wealth do not have any effect on happiness.

Building on Easterlin's findings is an array of subsequent research that has aimed to more directly examine the influence economic drivers may have on people's lives. Such research consistently demonstrates that those who place a high priority on achieving financial or materialistically oriented goals also report lower levels of personal life satisfaction, happiness and vitality, as well as higher likelihoods of experiencing symptoms of depression and anxiety.[5]

Amongst this research includes an influential paper published in the 1990s by Consumer Psychologists Marsha Richins and Scott Dawson, who revolutionarily defined materialism as a 'value' rather than a behaviour or personality variable.[6] Here, the researchers defined three different aspects of materialism, which included placing possessions and their acquisition at the centre of one's life (which they termed acquisition centrality), believing that possessions and their acquisition are essential to one's happiness (defined as possession-defined success), and considering possessions as a key criterion for judging a person's level of worth and success (defined as acquisition as the pursuit of happiness). Using these definitions to measure a group of US participants' attachment to materialistic beliefs and attitudes, they found that beliefs associated with these domains were negatively related to participants' life satisfaction and the quality of their relationships with others.

By defining materialism as a value (versus a specific behaviour or personality variable), Richins and Dawson's pioneering research provides us with the understanding that materialism goes beyond just the act of consumption and instead can be interpreted as a broader cultural ideal that can drive our aspirations and sense of identity. This conceptualisation inspired a range of subsequent research into the potential psychological consequences associated with highly orienting oneself towards materialistic values. Professor of Psychology at Knox College, Tim Kasser, has been at the forefront of much of this research. Kasser has dedicated a large part of his career to researching the psychological effects materialistic values can have on one's psychological health, as well as the other associated consequences that can come from fixating on materialistic pursuits. Kasser's early research saw him develop his *Aspirations Index*, which he uses to measure people's values and aspirations — and then classify these into either intrinsic or extrinsic domains.[7] He defines intrinsic values and aspirations as those relating to self-acceptance, being closely connected to one's family and friends, and a desire to work for the good of one's community. Extrinsic-based values, on the other hand, he defines as desires revolving around financial success, consumeristic goals and social recognition. Using these distinctions across a wealth of research studies, Kasser offers further evidence of how a high attachment to extrinsic and materialistic based goals can adversely affect an individual's everyday happiness, as well as different facets of their psychological health. His findings consistently point to a high attachment to materialistic values and behaviours relating to higher levels of depression, anxiety and poorer social relationships with others.[8]

Focusing on the social consequences an emphasis on materialism can lead to, Kathleen Vohs, a Professor of Marketing from the University of Minnesota, led an experiment exploring how people's attachment to money may influence their behaviours and attitudes towards others.[9] Here, the researchers conditioned one group of participants towards the idea of money by handing them thousands of dollars' worth of monopoly money, as well as by requesting that participants read essays on the joys of growing up with lots of money, while another group of participants were given no such priming. The researchers then provided both groups of participants with tasks whereby they could choose to work either independently or collaboratively with the other participants while also putting participants, in situations where they were given a choice to engage in prosocial and cooperative behaviours. Interestingly, the participants who were prompted to think about money were consistently more inclined to, as the authors put it, 'play alone' and 'work alone', showing they were less likely to request help from others while also less helpful toward others when compared to the participant group not conditioned towards ideas of money. From this finding, the authors conclude that reminders of money and the materialistic attitudes they foster can undermine goals and behaviours concerned with the welfare of others. This conclusion provides us with further insight into the link between materialistic values and poorer mental health outcomes, in that this connection may be explained by the isolating attitudes and behaviours inherent in materialistic lifestyles that are incompatible with our deeper psychological needs.

This connection between materialistic ideals leading to greater unhappiness, disconnection from others and poorer overall health outcomes is at odds with the prevailing modern notions of what is most important for a good life. Contrary to the lifestyles we see promoted to us via advertising campaigns, social media and television, the science instead shows us that pursuing these materialistic based objectives will ultimately have a detrimental effect on our psychological health and overall happiness. As Zygmunt Bauman writes, when we live life in pursuit of greater financial resources to fund our materialistic lifestyles, 'we do so at such incessant speed we are often seldom aware of the seriousness with which we need to urgently address the fact we are living on both borrowed money and time'.[10] Elaborating on this point, Bauman refers to the Red Queen's advice to Alice in Lewis Carroll's classic tale *Through the Looking Glass*: 'It takes all the running we can do just to keep in the same place' the Queen shares, 'that if we actually want to get somewhere else, well we must run at least twice as fast as that'. And so it often is when we orient our aspirations and lives around the attainment of materialistic pursuits that we commit to a never-ending and often unyielding cycle of needs.

Want Versus Need

All this is not to say that we should not set goals in pursuit of job promotions, purchasing our dream home, or even driving around in a nice new car. As the Dalai Lama states in *the Art of Happiness*, there is no harm in, for instance, desiring a car to help you manage your day-to-day dealings or a nice house to live in that can help provide you with financial stability.[11] What can be harmful, however, is when this want begins to manifest as greed. Greed, which the Dalai Lama defines as 'an exaggerated form of desire', often leads to an over-expectation of what the fulfilment of such a desire will bring about in one's life. When we 'over expect' in a materialistic sense, we essentially overstate the meaning behind a particular materialistic aspiration we may have. We may, for example, sacrifice a great deal to purchase a luxury car, thinking that this acquisition will lead us to experience greater happiness. We may really yearn for this car, but when that desire becomes a reality, and it is in our possession — whilst there may be a period of immense satisfaction — after a while, it is likely that this satisfaction will dissipate. At this point, perhaps even the desire for a newer car will arise. Another example might be that we may work tirelessly in pursuit of a greater job title that carries more recognition and status than our current role. We work avidly to reach this new position, placing large chunks of our hopes of future happiness and self-worth on its attainment. Yet once we finally arrive at the top of this mountain, metaphorically bloodied and bruised, we quickly realise that whilst the additional recognition and status that comes with this position is nice, the same problems we had in our life before are still there. In fact, when such a scenario is played out, the additional responsibility and pressure that often come with promotions can actually create even further complications for our lives. This mentality of 'if I could just get this next thing I am chasing, I will then be happy' and the subsequent disappointment that seems to come with actually meeting these desires is explained by the processes of what psychologists refer to as *hedonic adaptation* or the *hedonic treadmill* as it's otherwise termed. This is a psychological theory that essentially suggests that we constantly adapt to our material surroundings. Therefore, as our prosperity may increase, so do our expectations, with our level of happiness very quickly aligning with our newly acquired circumstances. So, the lesson here is quite clear. If you recently purchased a brand-new Mercedes-Benz, that's great. By all means enjoy it. But do so with a sense of contentment and gratitude, and not feelings of entitlement and a yearning for a Lamborghini! As the Greek sage Epictetus wrote as far back as 100AD: *'He is a wise man who does not grieve for the things which he has not but rejoices for those which he has'*.[12]

To summarise this chapter, I am reminded of a discussion I had with a man I met in the favelas of Rio De Janeiro, whom I will give the pseudonym of Lucas. After he had walked me and a small group of others through the favela that he had lived within for the majority of his life, Lucas and I got to talking about his experiences of growing up inside of it and the many dangers and challenges that came with it. In addition to the immediate issues of safety one is faced with within such an environment, life in a favela presents all sorts of resource-related challenges. As a start, these include frequent power outages, limited access to clean water, the cramped living conditions, and the financial difficulties many residents face in making ends meet. In spite of these challenges, across our discussion, Lucas evocatively recalled with extreme fondness his experiences of growing up in the favela and the many unique experiences he was immeasurably grateful for throughout his childhood. He shared fond memories of chasing around a soccer ball alongside other neighbourhood children in the limited street space the favela provided, of late-night surfing sessions with his friends and the enormous family he had come to form with his neighbours that living within such close quarters of one and another lent itself to, as well as the close proximity he had to the beautiful beaches and mountains of Rio De Janeiro from where his favela was situated.

As Lucas was sharing this, I was struck by the excitement and enthusiasm with which he recalled his upbringing. At no point throughout his discourse was there a tinge of resentment or bitterness at having been born into such abject poverty. This lack was particularly pronounced by the fact that only a short walk from Lucas's favela was a series of lavish beachfront homes and apartments that clearly exposed a very different side of life. There were no disparaging comments about the modest accommodation that he had grown up in and continued to live in today, the instability and danger living amidst an environment of heavy crime had brought to his life, nor a resentment towards whatever opportunities life in a favela may have deprived him. Instead, his story came across as one of fondness for having grown up around people who cared for him and, as he put it, the enormous family he has today that extends well beyond his immediate relatives, as well as an appreciation for the significant natural beauty that surrounds him in his home city. Essentially, he embraced the experiences of a life he had been able to share with the people most special to him in an environment that was equally meaningful to him.

Today, across the developed world, we are often presented with far more secure and favourable living conditions than in the favelas of Brazil. Beyond the obvious safety measures we enjoy, the comparative financial freedoms we benefit from allow us greater flexibility than ever before to make key life decisions and pursue the desires we have for our future. This is of course a wonderful thing. Yet more generally speaking, what Lucas's narrative teaches us is that when it comes down to what is most important and fulfilling in life and what moments will truly be archived amongst the collection of our most treasured memories, it is not the 'materialistic' based experiences we have that will be reflected on. Instead, it is the people we share life's everyday moments with and the excitement we may feel towards these everyday moments that counts. Would having grown up in the nearby mansions that lined the Rio De Janeiro boardwalk, complete with a private backyard, increased privacy and more reliable electricity, have added anything to Lucas's fond recollections of his upbringing? Certainly, there were opportunities Lucas had been deprived of and potentially moments of intense fear and tension he would have lived through based on the environment he was born into, but would his late-night surfing trips have been more glowingly recalled if he and his friends were catching waves on the newest available boards, or if their neighbourhood soccer games had taken place on perfectly manicured pitches whilst wearing the latest boots? For all the security, comfort, and resource-related benefits such a parallel upbringing would have meant for Lucas, based on what he shared, this alternate upbringing would likely have in actual fact deprived him of the joys that today make up the fond memories of his life. Undoubtedly, there was hardship and things that he had endured throughout his life in the favela that would be difficult for others to fully comprehend. Yet in spite of these challenges, what was evident in his description was a focus on what he did have, such as the people he got to share his experiences of life with and the feeling of being completely engaged in day-to-day life, rather than a perspective rooted in lack.

It is these pillars of spending time with our loved ones and the everyday moments we share with those closest to us that are most likely to lead to the memories that are really going to matter when we look back on our lives. And so it is with materialistic pursuits more generally. We can strive all we like to achieve greater financial wealth or a higher level of status throughout society. But when we reflect back upon our lives in our final hours, it will not be the things we managed to own that we reflect fondly over, nor will it be how many followers we may have on social media that comforts us. Instead, it will likely be the people we spent our life with, such as our family and friends, recollections of the peak experiences we have had across our lifetime, as well as the way we contributed to the lives of others around us, that will truly comfort us and allow us to know we have lived a good life. It is worth remembering this truth the next time you find yourself destroying yourself physically and mentally in order to keep up with the materialistic demands presented by our modern environment, all the while neglecting life's more important facets and potentially overlooking the many good things you likely already have in your life right now. As His Holiness the Dalai Lama teaches, the 'true antidote for greed is contentment'.[13]

****

Nearly two centuries after Volney Palmer set up the first US advertising agency, the materialistic focus of the developed world is showing no signs of slowing down. This would suggest that a large-scale social shift away from such ideals is unlikely in the near future. So, it instead really comes down to us as individuals to make choices. We can let these commercialised messages about what goods and lifestyle factors we need to live a good life influence our decisions and behaviours. Alternatively, we can adopt a more critical approach to these messages modern environments are sharing with us about what we 'need', and better understand what really is most important for a happy and contented life.

The Biblical Book of Ecclesiastes nicely sums up the folly of our materialistic desires. Written in approximately 500 BCE by an author who was clearly well-versed in the futility of materialism as a pathway to happiness, this book shares the following advice regarding materialistic pursuits:

> I increased my possessions, I built houses for myself, I planted vineyards for myself. I designed royal gardens and parks for myself, and I planted all kinds of fruit trees in them, I did not restrain myself from getting whatever I wanted. I did not deny myself anything that would bring me pleasure… Yet when I reflected on everything I had accomplished and on all the effort that I had expended to accomplish it, I concluded: All these achievements and possessions are ultimately profitless, like chasing the wind!' (Ecclesiastes 2, V4-6, V11, New English Translation).

With the advent of social media, modern culture is more active in the promotion of materialistic ideals than ever before, subsequently confusing our understanding of what makes for a good life, as well as where we should prioritise our attention. Yet by redirecting our focus towards a contentment and gratitude for what we already do have (and not what we lack), while simultaneously putting our attention towards the aspects of life that really do matter, such as our relationships with others and the things that truly fulfill us, we can foster a greater sense of peace and wellbeing within ourselves.

Chapter 5

The Pursuit of Happiness and its Discontents

> 'This lamentable phrase — the pursuit of happiness — is responsible for a good part of the ills and miseries of the modern world.'
> Malcolm Muggeridge

At the height of the Victorian literary era, British novelist Samuel Butler published his utopian science fiction classic, *Erewhon*.[1] Joining the echo of discontent towards nineteenth-century British society — which was the popular target of many other British writers of the time — Butler's idyllic city of Erewhon satirises the many social, political and technological changes that he saw as taking place in his English homeland. The story centres on the adventures of a sheep farmer named Higgs, who sets off on a journey from his pastoral home in pursuit of riches. During his travels, Higgs chances upon the land of Erewhon, where he is immediately charmed by both the natural beauty of the region as well as the physical beauty of its welcoming inhabitants. As the story develops, however, Higgs discovers a darker side to life in this village and its friendly appearance. He comes to learn that within the local Erewhonian law, instances of illness, misfortune and general unhappiness amongst the village's population are cruelly punished. As a sufferer of bronchitis is told by a judge in the *Misplaced Confidence Court*: 'Prisoner at the bar, you have been accused of the great crime of labouring under pulmonary consumption', with the accused sentenced to a lifetime of hard labour for spreading the subversive idea of hardship throughout the community. As Higgs's narration continues to unfold, it is revealed that the citizens of Butler's Erewhon perpetually give off the appearance of being happy not by choice but because such a façade is required by law.

The story of Erewhon outlines a rather terrifying dystopia, and yet, in parts, it acts as an interesting case study when we contemplate modern life in the Western world. Much like the society described by Butler, feelings of happiness are heavily prioritised across Western environments today. On the surface, this makes a good deal of sense. Research has shown that greater levels of personal happiness lead to better relationships with others, greater satisfaction with life and improved overall wellbeing. As such, many people living within Western cultural settings place a great emphasis on the pursuit of experiencing personal happiness as their prevailing emotional state. In some cases, such an environment can lead people to the belief that to be happy is to be normal, and any feelings otherwise are contrary to how we were designed to feel. Brock Bastian, a Professor of Psychology at the University of Melbourne, has written extensively on the ways in which Western cultural surroundings often reinforce ideals of happiness.[2] Bastian suggests this is the case specific to the extensive happy cues embedded in such environments. The seemingly perfect lives we see projected across social media channels, or the 'happily ever after' endings so common in Hollywood films, are just some of the many ways our culture reinforces ideals of happiness. Bastian's research and collected writings suggest that being surrounded by messages directing us towards ideals of happiness has the potential to lead us towards constantly pursuing feelings of happiness and, in turn, leave us with the understanding that feeling happy is our natural state of being. In response to this understanding, we can then come to subsequently direct our lives — inclusive of our aspirations, values, and behaviours — with the pursuit of happiness as our ultimate end goal.

This happiness-fixated environment that is so present across Western settings today, tends to largely centre on the 'emotion' of happiness, which can be understood as moment-to-moment feelings of pleasure, cheerfulness, or gratification. This differs from the deeper conceptualisation of happiness, which is reflected in a contended and meaningful life rather than fleeting emotion-based feelings. These are of course not mutually exclusive concepts, and yet psychological research has challenged the way we have come to conceptualise happiness in the Western world, indicating that over emphasising our want for emotional happiness, can actually lead us to experiencing less of it. Whilst this sounds incredibly contradictory, such research shows that expecting or desiring to feel happy all the time can in fact hinder the likelihood of us feeling this way, due in part to the way these expectations can lead us to perpetually 'monitor' our emotional state.[3] This process involves continuously evaluating our emotional state, and then contrasting how we may feel at any point in time with how we *think* we should feel. Much like the outcomes when we try not to think about something (and instead fixate our minds on exactly what it is we are trying not to think about!), emotional monitoring can in essence lead us to 'overthink' feeling happy, and place too much pressure on ourselves to feel a certain way, resulting in feelings of disappointment if our actual mood doesn't align with our desired emotional state.

Pursuing, Expecting or Overvaluing Happiness Makes us Miserable

Our expectations are understood to be a big factor in determining our emotional experiences of everyday life. A perhaps relatable example of this exists in our annual attempts to celebrate the bringing in of a new year. This is of course a celebration that sees many of us spend vast amounts of time and money trying to source out the best possible way to bring in the new year in style. And yet, despite these efforts, there is often an unspoken understanding that New Year's festivities are 'over-hyped', leaving revellers disappointed and let down if the reality of their celebrations doesn't meet the expectations they held for them.[4] Beyond suggesting that we shouldn't make such a big deal about New Year's Eve celebrations (although we likely always will), this example of our expectations for an enjoyable time and subsequent experiences of disappointment if these expectations aren't met, illustrates that when we chose to focus on and perpetually monitor our personal feelings of happiness, the less likely we are to actually experience it.

Wanting to explore the association between our expectations of happiness and subsequent experience of it, US Psychologists Jonathan Schooler and Dan Ariely led an experiment whereby participants were required to listen to a famous piece of music (Stravinsky's 'The Rite of Spring') and document their feelings of happiness as they did so.[5] One group of participants were instructed to try to really focus on enjoying the experience of the music and to maximise their happiness whilst listening to it, while the other group were given no instructions at all. This first group of participants was also asked to report how happy they felt during the listening period, while the other group was just asked to report on their happiness once the piece of music had finished. Interestingly, those who tried to maximise their happiness whilst listening to the music and who had been checked in on to see whether they were experiencing feelings of happiness reported significantly lower levels of happiness than those who weren't given any instructions at all. These findings highlight this paradox that can take place when we are overzealous in our pursuit of this in-the-moment happiness, in that the more pressure we place on ourselves to feel happiness at any given moment, the more likely we are to hinder this happening organically, leaving ourselves feeling disappointed if our happiness benchmark is not met.

It would seem that the consequences of this mismatch between our expectations for happiness and the subsequent realities of our lives, which can include an array of both good and bad emotional states, can set us up for failure. This is especially so when we engage in comparing our level of happiness with those around us. Iris Mauss, a Psychology Professor at the University of Denver, came to later term this phenomenon 'valuing happiness'.[6] According to Mauss, when we value happiness, we can come to set high and potentially unrealistic expectations of it for our lives. These are expectations that are oftentimes driven by the earlier mentioned societal norms of how we are told our lives should look, and yet are often expectations that are not compatible with our everyday experiences or emotional realities. Instead, these expectations can be counterintuitive for our happiness in that they can lead us to be self-critical if we feel we are not meeting the happiness benchmarks society sets for us, and resultantly question what we're doing wrong. In examining this idea, Mauss, along with a team of researchers, ran an experiment whereby one group of participants were asked to read a fake newspaper article discussing the importance of happiness while another group were given a neutral article that didn't mention happiness at all. Both groups were then asked to watch a happy film clip designed to encourage positive emotions. Interestingly, the participants who were required to read the article propagating happiness ended up reporting feeling more disappointed about their emotional state and reacted less positively to the emotion-inducing film clip than those who didn't read the pro-happiness article. Much like the conclusions reached by Schooler and Ariely, these findings led the authors to state that over-emphasising the importance of experiencing in-the-moment happiness can actually lead us to experience less of it.

Further research suggests that overvaluing the emotion of happiness creates challenges not only due to this mismatch between our expectations and reality, but also in how this cognition can impair our capacity to deal with our negative experiences and emotions. Austrian-born psychologist Edith Weisskopf-Joelson neatly outlined how this phenomenon may eventuate over half a century ago by writing: 'Our current mental-hygiene philosophy stresses the idea that people ought to be happy, that unhappiness is a symptom of maladjustment. Such a value system might be responsible for the fact that the burden of unavoidable unhappiness is increased by unhappiness about being unhappy'.[7] That is to say, when we normalise happiness as our default state of being, our negative emotions and experiences can come to be interpreted as obstacles to be avoided at all costs, rather than unescapable parts of the human experience.

Research led by Brock Bastian suggests that this social pressure to avoid feeling any negative emotions can actually intensify these very same negative emotional feelings.[8] Across a series of studies, Bastian and his research team found that in environments where participants were expected to be happy, they were more likely to reject their negative emotional states when they arose. This rejection led to participants actually experiencing heightened feelings of their negative emotions and poorer wellbeing outcomes more generally. Discussing these findings, the authors conclude that in surroundings where people are expected to be happy, people can consequently come to interpret their negative emotions as 'failure', a label that can subsequently exacerbate their felt discomfort even further. Further research led by Australian Psychologist Lucy McGuirk showed that people are more likely to self-punish and ruminate over failure in environments where happiness is portrayed as highly important and valuable.[9] Here, the researchers ran an experiment that had people try to complete a range of complex tasks (some which could be solved and some which could not) in one of two different rooms (one plain room and another fitted out with an array of posters and messages promoting happiness). Participants were then tasked with engaging in a brief breathing exercise. Their findings showed that the participants who had failed to complete their assigned task in the 'happy room' were far more likely to be distracted by ruminating on this failure during the breathing exercise than those who had experienced failure in the room without any happiness material. Significantly, the more participants ruminated on their inability to complete this task, the more intensely they experienced negative emotions in response to this. These findings suggest that when we experience a negative setback in an environment that overly promotes the feelings of happiness, it can lead us to feel far worse emotionally when compared with experiencing that same setback in an environment where happiness is not so heavily emphasised.

The 'Crime' of Unhappiness

While it is true that today's society does not look upon unhappiness as a crime as it did in Butler's fictitious Erewhon community, individually we still may perceive it as a crime worthy of self-punishment. Indeed, much like the Erewhonian society described earlier in this chapter, the way we have come to interpret happiness in Westernised environments has led to a perception that negative emotions should be interpreted as pathological in that they are removed from social norms. On the surface, this might not sound like such a bad thing, but negative emotions, including sadness, anxiety and fear, are generally quite painful and unpleasant in how we experience them. And yet, these negative emotional experiences are an inevitable and necessary part of normal psychological functioning, drawn upon when we are presented with the many challenging situations life can throw at us.

This idea of negative emotions being incompatible with how we have come to understand and conceptualise happiness is indeed very problematic. Even amidst times when modern life affords us so many comforts, from the climate-controlled homes we live in, to the amazing medications available to us that can promptly cure all sorts of ailments, suffering and hardship are inescapable, and at times, important aspects of the human experience. For thousands of years, religious and philosophical teachings have recognised this reality, often encouraging the embrace of pain and suffering, as well as the consequent negative emotions these experiences may evoke. Roughly 400 years BC, for example, Buddha talked about happiness in a way that highly contrasts with today's Western interpretation by stating that the path to happiness actually begins from an understanding of the root causes of suffering. The first of the four 'noble truths' (the core of Buddhist teaching around what makes for a meaningful life) outlines the term 'dukkha', which refers to the reality and importance of suffering within everyday life. These sufferings can include aging, illness, death, and the mundane nature of everyday life. According to Buddhist doctrine, these sufferings serve as a central tenet to the nature of our existence.[10] In the New Testament Book of James, the author teaches the importance of suffering for developing perseverance and character. Here it is written: 'consider it pure joy, my brothers and sisters, whenever you face trials of many kinds, because you know that the testing of your faith produces perseverance' (James 1:2, New International Version). More recently, nihilist Philosopher Friedrich Nietzsche developed an entire philosophical branch centred on the importance of suffering, famously stating that: 'Only great pain is the ultimate liberator of the spirit'. Contrary to our modern approaches to avoiding suffering, the major religions of the world, as well as many of the great philosophers, teach that suffering is both expected and necessary to make us human beings.

The Importance of Culture

Despite this time-tested wisdom, contemporary Western approaches to happiness communicate a message that people should strive for and prioritise their personal happiness above all else, leaving negative feelings such as sadness and disappointment as subsequent hindrances to this goal. Sociologists Edgar Cabanas and Eva Illouz suggest that this approach to happiness is defined predominantly around the absence and presence of certain emotional experiences. They write that this perception of feel-good happiness has: 'grown into a fundamental part of our understanding of ourselves and the world', adding that 'it feels and rings so natural today that to call happiness into question is odd if not audacious'.[11] Interestingly, this hedonic cultural approach to happiness is highly diverged from traditional Eastern cultural approaches. In Eastern cultures, suffering and negative affect are seen as inevitable elements of life, and instead of being avoided, they are embraced as tools necessary for personal growth.[12] Reflecting on these differing cultural interpretations of happiness, a study exploring the pursuit of happiness in differing cultural contexts led by Canadian-based Psychologist Brett Ford highlights the importance of broader cultural norms in determining how we may choose to define and, in turn, pursue happiness. Within the paper's introduction, the authors write: 'how we define happiness determines what we pursue when we 'pursue happiness' and should thus influence whether that pursuit is likely to be successful or not'.[13] Their findings go on to suggest that cultures that are socially more collectivistic, such as Eastern cultures, are more likely to encourage socially engaged experiences of happiness. Within these environments, happiness is likely to be defined as an outcome dependent upon strong social engagement with others, whereby people tend to seek happiness largely through social interactions and relationships. Korean psychologist and happiness expert Eunkook Suh argues that people from Eastern contexts tend to feel pressure to belong, and thus their lives are more guided by the need to have good interpersonal relationships than to be individually happy.[14] This is in contrast to people living within an individualistic culture, whereby people are instead more likely to define happiness in a more self-centred way, inclusive of pursuing one's own personal needs, aspirations and comforts, and would be far less inclined to seek happiness through social engagement.

Similarly, as discussed in the previous chapter, cultures that are highly oriented towards materialistic ideals tend to encourage aspirations and behaviours that are materialistic in nature. These aspirations can resultantly become deeply embedded in how one comes to define happiness, as well as how one chooses to pursue it. In a consumeristic culture, one might for instance, perceive an important criterion of happiness as including the achievement of certain material benchmarks compared to those around them. This may include being able to afford the latest 'it' goods or having a financial income that is equivalent, or indeed better, to the income of those around them. This stands in contrast to cultures whereby materialistic desires are less pervasive, and happiness is pursued more through the means of virtuous living, character development, and the building up of one's community. The pervasiveness of materialism within Western cultural interpretations of happiness is articulated well by Christian Smith and his team of sociologists in the conclusion of their study on the lives of young US people. Here, they suggest that the materialistic environment in which US people find themselves in the twenty-first century has led to an interpretation of happiness that is strongly connected to consumeristic outcomes. They reported that of the young people they interviewed for their study, more than half shared that their personal happiness could be measured by what they own and that buying more things would equate to making them happier.[15]

It is true that interpretations of happiness are always going to be ambiguous and subjective from culture to culture, as well as person to person. Therefore, creating a universal definition of happiness is fraught with difficulty, and rest assured that has not been the intention of this chapter. The intention has been to instead look at the concept of happiness as a highly desirable goal in Western environments and an emotion that is often misunderstood in a way that can be counterintuitive to our emotional wellbeing (and ironically, our happiness). So, what is the solution to this? As we have explored, overemphasising the need to feel happy, while subsequently shying away from any emotions contrary to this, can lead to problems. Yet by recognising and accepting the unrealistic nature of experiencing constant happiness, we can allow ourselves to be more aware of this happiness culture that surrounds us, and in the process, approach it in a more functional way. If successfully adopted, this approach can also equip us to be more accepting of our moment-to-moment emotional states, whether they be good or bad. If, for example, on a very ordinary Wednesday morning, you arrive at your place of work feeling tired and perhaps a little melancholy, only to be met with a work environment that perhaps isn't as exciting or dynamic as those you might see in your favourite television dramas, that's okay. Feeling mundane within everyday situations is a perfectly acceptable and normal state of being. Instead of questioning why we aren't happy and therefore what we are doing wrong in the midst of these everyday situations, famed

Humanistic Psychologist Abraham Maslow suggests a counter approach to negating our routine circumstances. Within his hierarchy of needs theory, Maslow proposed that personal fulfilment should be pursued through personal growth, a process he labels 'self-actualisation'. According to Maslow, self-actualising people perceive reality for what it is, and yet carry a sense of gratitude and 'continued freshness of appreciation' into their everyday life.[16] Specific to routine situations such as going into work, a 'self-actualiser' may seek out moments of appreciation throughout the day, perhaps by taking a moment to admire the view they have from their office window or by really cherishing a moment of conversation they have with a co-worker. Maslow states that people who successfully self-actualise: 'enjoy life in general and practically all its aspects, while most other people enjoy only stray moments of triumph', with this enjoyment applying even to the everyday tasks we are required to do as an inevitable part of life.[17] Thinking back to the example discussed earlier in this chapter of overestimating the amount of fun we may have celebrating New Year's Eve, if you are disappointed with a night spent celebrating with friends and loved ones, then something is wrong. Such a response shows a lack of gratitude towards the experiences you did have, as well as perhaps a 'grass is greener elsewhere' mentality that is not conducive to experiencing happiness. If we instead apply Maslow's model of self-actualisation to this situation, we are likely to carry a very different attitude to our experiences, whereby we deeply value the time we have for the little joys it may bring us, like the company we share, or the nice food we may eat.

Importantly, within his discourse on self-actualisation, Maslow also endorses the idea of 'growth' as a crucial factor in cultivating habits that can lead to a more enduring sense of happiness. Maslow suggests that if we are so perpetually focused on happiness, we may miss opportunities for growth through the inevitable sufferings and hardships life can bring. That is not to say we should not strive towards being 'happy', but rather we need to shift our understanding of what that actually means beyond just perpetual feelings of warmth and euphoria. Instead, we should strive towards living a life centred on the attainment of long-term happiness, inclusive of the hardships and uncomfortable emotions that may seem to be temporarily holding us back from it, and yet are actually likely to be important 'growth factors' that are necessary for its realisation. Specific to the example given earlier of suffering through a very ordinary workday, this growth mindset may be applied to one's working routine by knowing that such time spent labouring away is allowing for their children to be fed, their bills to be paid, and an overall sense of happiness to resultantly be experienced at a later date. This idea of pursuing 'later' happiness through experiences of growth was explored by US Psychologists Lahnna Catalino, Sara Algoe and Barbara Fredrickson. Here, the researchers observed that when people prioritise behaviours that maximise the likelihood of future happiness, rather than attempting to engage emotional feelings of happiness 'in the moment', they experienced an increase in positive emotions, higher levels of life satisfaction and reduced depressive symptoms.[18] Terming this approach to happiness 'prioritising positivity', they found that as opposed to the concept of valuing happiness described earlier in this chapter, pursuing happiness with future happiness in mind enables one to be less focused on moment-to-moment 'happy feelings', and instead focus on behaviour and growth factors that may lead to happiness at a later point in time.

These findings indirectly support Maslow's theorising that approaching happiness with a growth mindset and a mindful approach to everyday situations, can allow for a more applicable pathway to pursuing happiness. A number of studies have since replicated Catalino, Algoe and Fredrickson's findings, indicating that prioritising behaviours that maximise the likelihood of future happiness relates positively to wellbeing. These studies have also found that this approach can lead to improved relationships with others, as well as higher levels of self-compassion, resilience, and mindfulness. In one such piece of research, I, along with Rebecca Szoka and Brock Bastian of the University of Melbourne, also found that pursuing happiness via these means of seeking out positivity at a later date was not associated with the same avoidance of one's negative emotions, as can happen when people overvalue happiness.[19] Our findings across multiple studies pointed to the important role that how we perceive and handle our negative emotions plays in relation to the likelihood of us experiencing happiness. These results provide further evidence of some of the key fallacies embedded in prevailing Western approaches to happiness, in the way it can lead us to reject our negative emotional states while also advocating for a mechanism of pursuing a more sustainable form of happiness. One focused on delayed gratification that is better catered to the realities of our everyday lives.

As we can see, when we strive for happiness as the ultimate end, there are consequences attached. When we feel pressured to experience constant feelings of happiness and place too strong an emphasis on feeling this way, the research shows we may fail to achieve this aim by way of firstly trying too hard to 'upregulate' our emotional states in order to achieve feelings of happiness. Further, we may come to view our negative emotions and experiences as a sign that something is wrong with us, whereby much like the utopian society of Erewhon described earlier, we may come to feel as though we are falling short of the important societal benchmarks of happiness that surround us. The feelings of self-judgement and condemnation that may follow such thoughts can then take us even further away from the actual realisation of happiness. By better acknowledging this cultural myth that happiness is our natural state of being, we can unchain ourselves from the unrealistic expectations of unyielding happiness. Through a greater acceptance of our negative feelings of sadness, discomfort, and disappointment and the pursuit of behaviours and experiences that are important for our growth and wellbeing, we will be best placed to experience a more authentic happiness. One that transcends circumstance.

*****

As Russ Harris, author of the bestselling *The Happiness Trap*, explains, in Western contexts we lead our lives by many 'unhelpful and inaccurate' ideas about happiness — ideas widely accepted because 'everyone knows them to be true'.[20] As we have explored, these prevailing ideas and interpretations of happiness have powerful repercussions for a person's life, including their values, behaviours, and aspirations for the future, as well as the likelihood that they will actually be happy.

Reflecting on the two distinctly different meanings of happiness given at the beginning of this chapter, the emotional definition of happiness and the deeper definition outlining a contented and meaningful life. Modern Western cultural norms seem to have over-emphasised the significance of this first definition of in-the-moment happiness, which has subsequently hindered people's ability to achieve the latter characterisation of a more enduring semblance of happiness in their lives. As this chapter has explored, prevailing Western interpretations of happiness are heavily centred on experiencing moment-to-moment happiness, with this focus leading to a distorted rejection of negative experiences and emotions. This is an interpretation of happiness that is not conducive to our day-to-day lives or emotional realities. Whilst experiencing the emotion of happiness is a wonderful feeling, and one that should be thoroughly enjoyed when it arises, these emotions should not be confused with the pursuit of a 'happy' and meaningful life, and the consequent negative emotions, discomfort and mundane experiences that may exist as a part of that.

The drastically improved security, health, technological and economic conditions that exist in Western contexts today versus previous generations have meant that the pursuit of happiness has never been so accessible to so many. And yet, within this context it would seem we have come to drastically misunderstand and overestimate the virtues of happiness, and this, paradoxically, has caused us to suffer. If we, both personally and collectively, are to be truly happy, a greater understanding of the true causes and nature of happiness is required. To get to this point, it is necessary to understand the importance of gratitude, contentment, and the role of hardship and growth experiences. As Holocaust survivor and Psychologist Victor Frankl once wrote: 'it is the very pursuit of happiness that thwarts happiness'.[21] To therefore actually live 'happily ever after', we need to redefine happiness and the way we pursue it in a way more consistent with what the research and ancient wisdom tell us about happiness. This includes pursuing a life of meaning and one aimed at fostering long-term happiness outcomes rather than in-the-moment happiness gains. It includes acknowledging hardship and discomfort as an unfortunate reality of life and a reality that is sometimes necessary for the optimisation of long-term happiness goals. Lastly, we should aspire to live a life that takes moments of mindfulness to express gratitude for the pleasantries of life we are presented with. This should not be done in a forceful way, but the next time we catch a glimpse of a well-formed rainbow taking shape outside our bedroom window, or find ourselves enjoying a meal with friends, take some time to appreciate that moment. If positive emotions happen to follow, that is a sign of authentic happiness.

Cultural Deceptions: How progress is making us miserable and how we can get back on track

Chapter 6

Reimagining Wellbeing

'As you ought not to attempt to cure the eyes without the head, or the head without the body, so neither ought you to cure the body without the soul.'
Plato

Between the years of 1959 and 1961, the people of the People's Republic of China were to endure one of the great tragedies of the twentieth century. Implementing drastic overhauls to the economic, social and agricultural practices of his country, Communist Party Chairman Mao Zedong began a relentless push to increase his country's exports.[1] These reforms were propagated to the Chinese people under the guise of the 'Great Leap Forward' campaign, a movement designed to rapidly propel the country towards the highly industrialised nation its leadership desired it to be. To support these objectives, radical changes to farming processes were undertaken in order to increase the quantity of harvest yields available for export. These modifications included revising 'archaic' agricultural methods in favour of evolving cutting-edge farming practices, as well as moving farmers onto collective farms, a system that allowed the Government to more closely monitor workers' output, while also ensuring the entirety of their harvest was directed towards the State.

As was the intention, these changes to the country's farming practices led to an increase in harvest yields, allowing China to more than double its grain exports at this time.[2] And yet, despite these impressive trade figures, the Chinese people, and in particular the working majority, suffered dearly. In order to meet these increased export targets, workers were forced to work significantly longer days, all the while being allocated little to no rations of their own harvests to live off. These circumstances eerily mirrored those of the Holodomor famine that had taken place in Ukraine some 30 years prior. Yet despite such lessons of history, Chinese officials and workers alike were similarly reluctant to speak out against these injustices for fear of imprisonment. Criticising the party regime was a very serious crime for the Chinese people at the time. Tragically, before long, these intense working conditions, lack of allocated food rations, and the silences that surrounded them were to culminate in a wave of famine that spread right across the country. In what became known as the Great Chinese Famine, Mao's 'Great Leap Forward' led to an estimated fifteen to forty million Chinese citizens dying of starvation, and thus the largest famine in human history.

Suffering Amid Abundance

Despite these atrocities being hidden from the rest of the world at the time by way of propaganda and misinformation, historians now possess a relatively sound understanding of the inner workings of the crisis. History today tells this as a story of how a country's drive for overly ambitious targets of agricultural and industrial production created the conditions for millions of Chinese people to be stripped of their own harvests and consequently left to starve. This catastrophe is especially tragic when we consider that it took place within the context of an exported food surplus. A surplus that was likely sufficient to feed the entire population. Chillingly, despite possessing such significant food resources, the Government's desire for productivity and economic superiority starved millions of its own people to death.

This level of human suffering, in spite of the necessary resources to preclude it, is an immensely troubling (if not terrifying) thought. People living within democratic contexts can today be thankful that such atrocities of mismanagement are unlikely to manifest themselves within such settings anytime soon. Over the past half-century, such environments have prioritised and pursued policies aimed at enhancing citizens' quality of life and, in general, have succeeded when measured by health and financial metrics, education levels, and individual freedoms. As discussed repeatedly throughout the previous chapters, the resources afforded to people across the developed world today allow unparalleled opportunities for a larger number of people than ever before to live a flourishing life. And yet, despite these increases in resources, opportunity and personal freedoms, there exists a disconnect between these developments and the psychological health of people living in these environments. Environments whereby people are themselves 'suffering amidst abundance'. This is a suffering that is of course, far more subtle than the agonising hurt brought on by starvation. However, it is a suffering that is similarly taking place against the backdrop of surplus resources available for people to thrive when it comes to their psychological health. In lauding the many progresses of the modern world, Cognitive Psychologist Stephen Pinker notes when it comes to personal happiness and wellbeing, 'we could do better'.[3] Given this disconnect between improvements to people's quality of life and the subsequent decreases in their psychological wellbeing and happiness, a deeper critique of what exactly constitutes health and wellbeing is needed.

What is health?

When considering what it means to be healthy, both individually and collectively, our conceptualisation of wellness is very much shaped by society's standards of what this entails. To this point, Psychologist John Christopher argues that interpretations of wellbeing are essentially culturally rooted 'ethical visions' based on one's judgment about what it means to be well.[4] On the back of the wondrous advances in medical science throughout the past century, expectations of wellness across most of the developed world today have far transcended those of days gone by. Over the past few decades, the significant evolutions in medical science, technology and pharmaceuticals have led to the elimination and prevention of an array of diseases and symptoms of ill-physical health that would have been quite unimaginable only a century ago. This progress has generated immense improvements to health outcomes worldwide and, with them, a subsequent dramatic increase in people's quality of life. Yet, as we have moved towards these significant advancements in health science, we seem to have simultaneously moved away from an appreciation of the many broader social elements that make up its foundations.

The definition of health offered by the World Health Organisation, amidst its establishment in 1948, serves as an example that can help illuminate this shift: 'Health is a state of complete physical, psychological and social wellbeing and not merely the absence of disease or infirmity'.[5] From this definition, we may infer a holistic understanding of wellbeing, comprising its physical, psychological, and social elements. More recent conceptualisations of health within academic and policy-related spheres are today largely dismissive of the non-physical elements of health offered by the WHO's classification, even going so far as to condemn it, with one such critique suggesting such a definition is more closely related to 'happiness' than 'health'.[6] Such critiques suggest definitions of health should instead more strictly capture the absence of disease and symptoms of ill-physical health as the core principle and barometers of good health. This streamlined interpretation of health is largely how we have come to frame health and wellbeing in contemporary Western environments. Here, wellbeing is largely quantified by 'hedonic' means. Hedonic wellbeing is defined predominantly as the absence of pain, discomfort and negative emotional experiences. This differs from the 'eudaimonic' perspective of wellbeing, which is a more abstract approach to wellbeing focused on fostering one's spirituality, virtuous and purposeful living, and close relationships with others. Eastern cultures are broadly understood to be eudaimonic-centred in their approach to health when compared to Western environments, which tend to be dismissive of these broader aspects of health. These narrower and reductionist hedonic approaches to health have led us to lose a deeper understanding of what it means to be holistically well. If we disregard a person's mental health, their satisfaction with life, and the deeper social and spiritual frameworks necessary for optimal wellbeing outcomes, we have little prospect of achieving this holistic wellness.

This contemporary understanding of health is a reality that is far removed from its original Old English definition. The term 'hælth' as it was originally scribed described the state and the condition of being completely sound or whole.[7] More precisely, good health was considered to be not only robust physiological functioning but psychological, social and spiritual soundness as well. As medical science evolved across the twentieth century, these more comprehensive characterisations of health began to be challenged and substituted by more narrow ones, such as the absence of physical illness and disease. Such a transition has unquestionably pushed our understanding of physical health forward, allowing it to be measured via objective and determinate quantities, streamlining research efforts towards the reduction of disease, illness and pain, and in turn, leading to more advanced approaches to physical health outcomes. And yet, when we think about the many different factors that make up good health and wellbeing, we can begin to see that a narrow encapsulation of health is insufficient to gauge whether one is truly flourishing.

Wanting to reconcile these early philosophical notions of health with our modern scientific understanding, American Psychologist Carol Ryff endeavoured to provide a more comprehensive notion of what constitutes wellbeing that went beyond just mere biological descriptions. Based on an extensive review of the philosophical and scientific literature on what made up wellbeing, Ryff set out to develop a measure that could scientifically capture the different psychological and social facets that make up wellbeing. Here, Ryff identified six core dimensions of wellbeing, including self-acceptance, positive relations with others, personal autonomy, a feeling of competence, a sense of meaning in life, and continued personal growth, with these dimensions forming the basis for what has become one of the most well-used measures of wellbeing within the psychological literature.[8] Curiously, however, despite its significant scholarly impact, Ryff's framework has not had as substantial an effect on the broader societal discourse about what it means to be holistically well today. A body of research emphatically links the various factors proposed by Ryff, including personal growth, meaning in life, and social connectedness, as critically important for achieving good psychological health, and their neglect is highly damaging to it. As Canadian health researcher Jonathan Lomas shares, when it comes to wellbeing: 'individuals cannot be understood by looking inside their bodies and brains; one must look inside their communities, their networks, their workplaces, their families and even the trajectory of their lives'.[9] Yet in spite of this understanding, Western notions of health continue to largely abide by 'hedonic' judgements, including the prevention of pain, discomfort and disease.

The Wrong Scorecard

It is of course true that the broader social contributors to health and wellbeing can be difficult to accurately gauge and measure. Consequently, these aspects are often overshadowed by measures that can be more easily quantified, such as the absence of disease. One further measure that is often linked to wellbeing, is a person's or country's level of financial wealth. As touched on in previous chapters, the connection between adequate financial means and quality of life is very real, especially when we consider the indisputable effects that higher levels of wealth have on the key health indicators of a society as well as an individual. And yet, too narrow a focus on economic growth at a political level, as well as personal income at an individual level, is only one component on the road to both flourishing individuals and a flourishing society. As articulated by the Easterlin Paradox, beyond a certain threshold, increasing wealth has minimal effect on wellbeing outcomes. Despite this understanding, economic performance metrics, such as a nation's GDP, continue to be widely used as general indicators of wellbeing. With such an emphasis placed on economic security as an essential accomplice to a society's health, the trickledown effect of this at a personal level is that we, as impressionable beings, have come to overestimate the amount of wellbeing associated with high levels of income. When we subsequently think that our own 'financial health' is more important than our emotional, mental or even physical health, we can engage in behaviours such as taking on longer work hours, which can actually have a detrimental effect on our wellbeing. When we abide by this idea, we can quickly become deprived of a range of the broader and more abstract elements of wellbeing, in exchange for the pursuit of greater financial security for our own lives. As stated by Australian economists Clive Hamilton and Richard Denniss, in wealthy societies, people often fail to distinguish what they 'want' from what they actually need.[10] Findings from a study I conducted alongside several research collaborators exploring how differing cultures conceptualised wellbeing, hint at this overstatement of 'want' versus need within Western perspectives of wellbeing.[11] Here, we conducted a series of interviews with participants from Chilean, Indian, Russian and Australian backgrounds, asking questions on how they personally defined wellbeing in the context of their own lives, as well as the importance they placed on the emotional, social, spiritual and financial aspects in contributing to it. Our findings showed that the Australian participants interviewed were far more likely to mention a good level of income as an important aspect of fostering their wellbeing, frequently pointing to its significance in allowing for 'important' lifestyle freedoms. This was a response not given by the Indian, Chilean or Russian participants, who instead largely indicated that financial resources were either unimportant in contributing to their sense of wellbeing, or only important in so far as allowing access to their basic needs to be sustained. Interestingly, the Australian respondents also highlighted the importance feelings of happiness held as an important component of their wellbeing, a view not held by the other cultural groups present in the study, who were more concerned with emotional and spiritual growth as pivotal components for their wellbeing.

Within his Nicomachean Ethics, Aristotle, as far back as the fourth century BC, stated that: 'the goal of life isn't feeling good, but is instead about living virtuously'.[12] Whilst many people today may agree with these sentiments, the application of such teachings can be heavily overshadowed by the overwhelming demands and allures of twenty-first-century life. These demands and pressures can consequently divert our attention away from these seemingly less urgent facets of health and instead lead us to only consider our health when we may be physically impaired by it in some way. Yet it was these deeper and more nuanced conceptualisations of health that prevailed across the West right up until the European enlightenment era, whereby amidst a very challenging landscape to one's physical and psychological health, sustaining one's social, emotional and spiritual health was amongst the core principles of good health. One could argue that such an approach may have served as an essential coping mechanism in such times. This was after all an environment whereby the majority of the European population were peasants, often living amidst immensely challenging living and working conditions. Threats to one's safety were also never far away. Religious and political oppression was rife, a swarm of diseases prevailed in taking the lives of both the young and the old, and if you were lucky enough to survive all of that, you could expect to fulfil the life expectancy course of around 45 years of age. Reflecting on these harsh realities provides us with a stark reminder of how far we have progressed, both medically and socially, beyond such circumstances. Nevertheless, it seems foolish to think we would advance so far only to create health issues for ourselves based on how we choose to live our lives. Now that so many have the opportunity, both financially and socially, to navigate their lives in a myriad of different directions, to consequently become ignorant of the historical wisdom on the importance of living a holistically healthy life seems an absurd waste of such immense progress.

To this day, many Indigenous Australian communities abide by an ethos of holistic health which encompasses one's mental, physical and spiritual health, and reflects an approach that in some ways parallels the values that once prevailed across pre-Enlightenment Europe.[13] For thousands of years, Indigenous Australians understood health as not just the physical wellbeing of an individual but also the social, emotional, and cultural wellbeing of the whole community. For many native Australian communities, this rounded understanding of health and wellbeing also incorporates broad issues like social justice, equity, and rights, as well as traditional knowledge and a connection to one's country.

Many Westerners today could learn a lot from this broader conception of wellness. Our lives may often look 'healthy' from the outside, but that does not always mean that they are. Across the developed world today, complete with its highly developed health metrics and conceptualisations of what it means to be well, we seem to have become negligent to simple yet crucial pieces of the wellbeing puzzle. This lack seems particularly the case in relation to the development of one's 'spirit', as ambiguous a term as it may be. A great drawback of this has been that traits universally associated with the idea of one's spirit — including resilience, hope, purpose and the pursuit of wisdom — have taken a back seat to the seemingly more pressing matters of our physical health and propensity to seek out comfort for our lives. We would indeed do well to heed these earlier discussed ideas of philosophical thought, religion and science that advocate for a more holistic conceptualisation of wellness. By better acknowledging these broader aspects of wellbeing, as well as what behaviours and values make these up, we are better positioned to genuinely foster it in our lives. As stated by Aristotle's favourite pupil, Plato: 'The reason why the cure of many diseases is unknown to the physicians of Hellas is because they are ignorant of the whole, which ought to be studied also; for the part can never be well unless the whole is well'.[14]

****

The atrocities of the Chinese Great Famine provide us with a highly sombre and yet poignant example of what happens when we divert the resources we do have away from nourishing our most basic needs. The lesson here is clear. We can starve in the midst of plenty. When we, either personally or societally, misunderstand what facets best equate to a holistic sense of wellbeing, all the while misallocating the resources we do have to achieve good health in ways not conducive to it, we ultimately suffer. As Richard Eckersley writes, 'we need to change the myths, beliefs and values by which we define ourselves, our lives, and what it means to be a wellbeing'.[15] Today, we understand health is governed by a complex interplay of biological, genealogical, and neurological factors. Beyond these features, however, there is also a range of broader social, psychological, and spiritual elements that are highly influential on our wellbeing. The available evidence shows that fostering close relationships with others, belonging to a community and engaging in rewarding work are all part of what makes up good health and wellbeing. Today, we have a greater opportunity than ever before to freely pursue these avenues for a holistic sense of health. And yet, perhaps in part due to a fundamental misunderstanding of what good health truly is, we make lifestyle choices — choices often influenced by our cultural surroundings — that can be harmful to it.

Reverting our understanding back towards a more encompassing definition of health across society, such as the outline proposed by the WHO some seventy years ago, would likely encourage us to better frame our behaviours, aspirations and lifestyles in ways that are consistent with achieving this more holistic sense of wellbeing. Alongside all the wondrous advances we have made to health outcomes across the past century, we need to transform our interpretation and understanding of health and wellbeing back towards the social elements that helped foster it in what were much more severe and challenging contexts to that which we live amidst today. To sell ourselves short of realising this rounded sense of wellbeing through mis-prioritising our time and energy on things that actually detract from it would be a gross injustice to the amazing progress we are fortunate enough to live amongst today, as well as the people that made them possible.

Part 2

Towards Change

Chapter 7

Lessons from a Pandemic

> 'How wonderful it is that nobody need wait a
> single moment to change the world.'
> Anne Frank

In December of 2019, the first case of COVID-19 was identified in the Chinese city of Wuhan. What would follow over the ensuing months was a global health pandemic, the likes of which were completely unprecedented in the modern developed world. Along with the immediate threat it posed to people's health, the COVID-19 pandemic generated a context of extreme uncertainty, worry and tension in ways unseen throughout the twenty-first century. Attempts to prevent the spread of the virus saw extraordinary 'lockdown' measures implemented globally, resulting in millions of people being either forced or strongly encouraged to stay at home. Suffice it to say the virus sent the world into a state of chaos socially, politically and economically.

From a psychological health perspective, the impact of COVID-19 and the measures used to contain it led to heightened experiences of fear, stress and anxiety for people the world over. Such a mass threat to people's mortality and health was completely foreign in the twenty-first century developed world. And whilst wealthier nations held several advantages in responding to the pandemic from both a health and economic perspective, it was also readily apparent that flourishing GDP rates and economies would not eradicate the health-specific challenges of the virus. As often happens during difficult times, the pandemic, along with all of the uncertainty and challenges it brought with it, exposed the modern world to a range of shortcomings. Indeed, this time of pandemonium made it apparent that the twenty-first-century Western world we have inherited, along with the lifestyles, attitudes and behaviours it drives, were not the ideals we had been led to believe they were.

At the individual level, the impact of the pandemic cruelly revealed these untruths in a number of contrasting ways. Those who prioritised their investment portfolios ahead of everything else in their life saw global markets plummet and with them their hard-earned assets. Those who had overly prioritised pursuing their personal happiness via the means of 'good times', were left with streaming services and books as some of the few ways to source that very same happiness as they languished in lockdowns. And despite heart-warming stories occurring globally of people going out of their way to help others through such difficult circumstances, those who desperately needed support throughout the pandemic — be it social support or otherwise — were often found left wanting amidst the individualistic culture that prevails across the Western world. Throughout the pandemic, people were placed in a situation whereby they could no longer rely on some of the 'modern ideals' discussed in this book to make sense of their lives. Due to the lockdown restrictions implemented the world over, people were not able to party until late to forget about their troubles. With warnings of a dire recession also imminent, people were forced to be more prudent with their finances and thus had to restrict their spending on the consumer items that they had become accustomed to. Instead, people were largely left with 'intrinsic' means to nurture their psychological health. When afforded time for recreational activities, one could, for example, spend time with their partner, their housemate or their family. They could devote an extended amount of time in the kitchen preparing a meal, or reengage with hobbies that had perhaps been left dormant for long periods of time — such as dusting off their guitar or picking up their paintbrush for the first time in years. From a social perspective, people were also required to employ more 'collectivistic' mindsets towards the people around them in order to help their community remain functional and safe. Essentially, this pandemic forced a large portion of people to engage in behaviours more focused on what really matters to both themselves as well as those around them.

A further byproduct of these novel and challenging times was that many people were left with more time than usual to think and reflect on their lives, leading to the contemplation of big questions, such as whether the life they had been living was truly satisfying to them. This reflection gave room for matters such as the increasing prevalence of mental health issues that were emerging across the developed world to receive much greater attention within both the minds of individuals as well as amongst popular discourse. As this problem was unpacked, a growing critique was thrust upon the culture we had been building for a number of generations in the Western world and a consensus that the environment we had fostered may have been contributing to these issues of psychological health.

Taken collectively, the findings discussed in the previous chapters point to elements of modern cultures, along with the mindset and behaviours they perpetuate, as presenting challenges to our mental health. In consideration of this, the aim of this chapter is to explore ways we can better navigate this challenging cultural landscape that surrounds us in twenty-first-century life. Specifically, what changes can be implemented at a social as well as personal level within this context in order to optimise our wellbeing and quality of life? Given the interconnected nature of the established cultural behaviours, attitudes and beliefs discussed so far, this chapter will explore potential societal-level changes to these issues from a broader, holistic perspective. In light of evidence showing the psychological harm of

Transforming Society

One of the most effective ways to better navigate the challenging cultural environment that surrounds us today, includes introducing society-wide efforts to help people better understand what core values, behaviours and ways of living truly support positive mental health outcomes. Specific to this idea, Tim Kasser states that psychologists rarely examine the effects that economic and sociocultural systems have on people's psychological health.[1] Kasser adds that as a result of this, efforts to treat symptoms of depression and anxiety have largely focussed on doing so at the personal level. With symptoms of ill-mental health such a subjective and personal experience, this individual approach is of course essential. Yet in addition to this method, he argues that addressing the broader social, cultural and lifestyle-based issues that are contributing to people's mental health challenges would likely help alleviate at least a portion of these symptoms of distress experienced by people today. This could also offer a more scalable method to better equip people with effective coping mechanisms as they endure such symptoms. Discussing the possibility of large-scale social campaigns that could be effective in achieving these aims, Kasser continues to suggest that the task of changing the culture and the perpetuated norms of society can seem 'overwhelming'.[2] With prevailing cultural traits deeply ingrained into the everyday social environment they shape, the prospects of mass societal change can indeed seem out of reach. However, as is the case with any widespread social issue, there are broad blanket systemic approaches that could help reduce the adverse effects these influences are having on people's lives today as well as the lives of future generations.

People are today seemingly indifferent to the philosophical and theological wisdom that has for centuries advocated for teachings and principles at odds with some of the cultural ideals that shape our lives today. As a highly rational society, we are however generally responsive to information backed by science, particularly when this information relates to one's health. Indeed, Kasser along with many other scholars, has suggested that people often begin making changes to their life by reflecting on research findings related to wellbeing. An example of this exists in a breakthrough medical study undertaken in the 1950s by American researchers Cuyler Hammond and Daniel Horn, which focussed on the causes of their death for men with a history of regular cigarette smoking. The findings, published in the *Journal of the American Medical Association*, led the authors to the following conclusion: 'It was found that men with a history of regular cigarette smoking have a considerably higher death rate than men who have never smoked or men who have smoked only cigars or pipes'.[3] This conclusion began to fuel anti-smoking rhetoric across the US, inclusive of health agencies advocating for people to quit smoking and policies shifting to dissuade people from the use of cigarettes. Within a decade of Hammond and Horn's study being published, smoking decreased in the US by thirty percent. Today, instances of smoking across the globe have dropped by more than seventy per cent since the publication of these findings.

We nowadays have a very firm understanding of the link smoking tobacco has with increasing one's risk of lung disease as well as a range of other ailments. Research findings linking cultural values and behaviours to psychological health outcomes are of course a little more tenuous in their clarity. However, the evidence we have reviewed throughout this book provides us with a relatively clear picture between the prevailing ways we have come to socialise, what we aspire to and how we choose to pursue both happiness and health, and their link to poorer psychological health outcomes. As we can see from the significant public response given to these findings on tobacco use and physical health, when a society comes to understand scientific research, it tends to be more critical of its attitudes and behaviours based on what this evidence is telling it. This is of course not exclusively the case, but generally speaking, scientific findings enable us to make more informed choices about what is best for our health and overall quality of life. A stronger societal understanding of the consequences associated with heightened individualistic social tendencies, would likely lead some people to rethink their social behaviours and attitudes, and better prioritise their time and attention towards creating stronger social networks which are crucial in nurturing good psychological health. As well as tobacco use, we have seen recent positive changes to people's energy usage and environmental practices in response to messages about the increasing harm to our planet caused by pollution and the human footprint. Similarly, broad social approaches to health have proven to be successful in overcoming prevailing attitudes towards other detrimental health behaviours, including poor dietary habits and sedentary lifestyles. These are all behavioural shifts that are not revolutionary, and yet we often need continued reminders to do the things that are good for us as well as our surrounding environment, irrespective of how obvious they may be. It is one thing to know the importance of maintaining a good level of social interaction with others. It is another to do so amidst a particularly busy week or difficult times. Essentially, social messaging better caters to the formation of positive habits, even when such habits may be an inconvenience. We humans are stubborn. However, with enough reinforcement, we are more likely to respond in ways that are best for us. Facilitating a better societal understanding of the lifestyle and behavioural factors shown to be most connected with our innate psychological needs would be a significant step in leading people towards experiencing better mental health.

Over the past few decades, countless corporate and community-based organisations have emerged across the globe with the intention of both destigmatising mental health issues and encouraging people to be more proactive in looking after their psychological wellbeing. Some of the key successes of these organisations include making information on what good mental health looks like more accessible, encouraging people to seek help if they are facing mental health challenges, and promoting practical strategies, such as the use of mindfulness meditation as a tool to reduce stress and anxiety. With research clearly outlining the connection between well-established social support networks and good psychological health, perhaps such organisations could also start to place more emphasis on encouraging people to better engage with their community as a means to help curb symptoms of loneliness, increase feelings of social support and in turn improve people's mental health. With community organisations today often finding themselves in desperate need of extra members, volunteers and supporters, such an initiative would have the dual benefit of strengthening such community groups as well as reducing the increasing rates of isolation that have become an unintended byproduct of overly individualistic cultures. Specific to the materialistic culture that surrounds us and the adverse beliefs and behaviours these environments can foster, recent research shows that encouraging people to reflect on 'intrinsic' based behaviours and goals while also critiquing consumer culture can reduce their attachment to materialistic pursuits and subsequently improve their wellbeing.[4] Mental health organisations and clinicians alike would therefore do well to better encourage people towards prioritising behaviours that focus on building strong relationships with others, pursuing personal growth and making a positive contribution to society as a key means to promoting better psychological health across our society.

Consistent with these aims, a group of economists from the UK established what they titled *A Wellbeing Manifesto for a Flourishing Society*, which highlights a number of key social changes they deem necessary for a society to achieve better mental health.[5] As part of their manifesto, they called for fostering wellbeing to become the primary role of government, suggesting politicians should be more focused on policies that cater for positive wellbeing outcomes for their citizens, and not just the economic ones that are often overemphasised. Here they argue that the success of governments should be more vigilantly assessed by the wellbeing experienced by the population they are governing — an outcome they argue could be tracked via annual measurements — rather than relying too much on economic indicators. Further to this, their manifesto urges governments to enact changes to the way education is delivered as an essential step in improving the wellbeing of society. Schools and Universities are increasingly driven by test scores, rankings, and career readiness, often at the expense of delivering education based on developing young people's character, sense of resilience and understanding of the world around them. This neglect towards the broader personal development of young people in the education sector has a number of key consequences. It can leave a young person without a well-established sense of direction while also leaving them unclear on what their core values may be. With such a lack of attention in mainstream curriculums on developing an individual's sense of self, it should come as little surprise that people become so drawn towards framing their hopes for the future around culturally reinforced ideals, such as those materialistic in nature, pursuing careers and forming identities that look to fulfill these. Drawing on these recommendations from the UK towards better societal wellbeing, a group of Australian economists proposed their own version of a 'wellbeing manifesto', specific to an Australian context. Here, the authors similarly encourage a shift in the education system from its hyper-focus on achievement and performance to instead focusing on young people's 'physical, emotional and moral wellbeing'.[6] As stated within this Australian manifesto for wellbeing, there is substantial evidence indicating that 'happy' people learn more effectively and that a person's wellbeing has a greater bearing on their enduring sense of quality of life than one's academic successes or credentials. Indeed, whilst a focus on achievement and career vocations may serve a nation's economy well, insofar as it prepares people to work in roles that support its growth, such an emphasis does so at the substantial cost of developing well-rounded people who are equipped for all that life may throw at them. Evidence of this 'transactional' style approach to education, whereby young people are developed for jobs ahead of life, can be seen in Australia itself, where a recent Parliamentary Bill was passed increasing the costs associated with studying a humanities degree, with the intention of coercing students towards study programs deemed to best serve the needs of the Australian job market. And yet, the study of the humanities, that is, the study of what it means to be human, was the very undertaking that early Universities were largely founded upon.

Surely amidst an increasingly digital world, exploring the essence of humankind is as valuable a pursuit today as it was back then? This exchange of what we could term 'human centred' education for strictly vocational education is undoubtedly complicit in the earlier mentioned declining interest in philosophy, theology and spirituality amongst Western populations. A greater focus on education providers delivering more space for young people to question life and its most important facets would likely lead to a better understanding and acceptance of who they are as individuals, help develop their character and morality, and assist in the understanding of what makes up a flourishing life. Better nurturing young people towards the realities of life while encouraging them to deeply question the world around them as well as what is most important to them is a vital step in improving the mental health of future generations.

Lessons from the Past, Prospects for the Future

The prospect of changing the cultural norms that surround us can again seem like a very challenging prospect if not a completely unrealistic one. Yet when we reflect on some of the historical shifts that have shaped the distinct cultural customs that today seem so normal to us, we can see that culture, however rigid, is transformable, ever shaped by changing influences. Discussing cultural changes of the past as an exemplar of the possibility of cultural change in the future, Richard Eckersley reflects on the enlightenment period of transition that took place across Western Europe between the late seventeenth and early nineteenth centuries.[7] This was of course a period of great social change, as people began to shift away from religious thought and embrace a more rational worldview. These significant changes are today widely understood as a response to the growing disenchantment across Western Europe towards religious and monarchial institutions, coupled with an increasing scientific curiosity that these institutions often sought to suppress. As cases of ill-mental health and dissatisfaction continue to rise, similar critiques of modern life and what it tells us is most important may increasingly emerge as they did extensively throughout the time of the Covid-19 pandemic. Eckersley argues, such critiques could lead to another large-scale change to the way people think and behave in such settings. This time however, perhaps the shift will see us revert more towards ways of living from the past rather than the new, in terms of were we focus our attention and time. These changes could include a return to better engaging with our surrounding communities, prioritising our relationships with others ahead of our motives for personal success, and better focusing our time on nourishing our deeper psychological and spiritual needs ahead of diving into another scroll through social media. This should not be done in a way that is regressive regarding the giant steps forward we have made as a society, such as the enlightenment of our scientific understandings and approaches. Rather, we should pursue this change in a way whereby we leverage all the good that exists within modern life to our advantage while understanding the limits of individual autonomy, materialistic pursuits, and the role of happiness in our lives. As Eckersley writes, 'greater awareness and acknowledgement of the flaws and failings of material progress and modernisation, however, can encourage us to think more positively about alternative ways of living which deliver a high quality of life, with much lower material consumption and social complexity'.[8]

Given how far modern societies have progressed from a medical, technological and economic perspective, we may as a result of these progressions be less inclined to critically reflect on any shortcomings of our current cultural environment when compared to days of old. Yet, as Zygmunt Bauman describes, when it comes to societal changes, 'there are no gains without losses'.[9] For all the social, technological and health-related improvements that have taken place across the past century and the many ways these mediums have drastically enhanced our lives, there have indeed been losses in exchange. For us to truly flourish in modern times, it's important these improvements do not make us dismissive towards the wisdom embedded in approaches to doing life of the past that were deprived of such progress, as well as present cultures that may resist them, and instead maintain more traditional approaches to life.

As an example of the latter, I fondly remember travelling through the country of Georgia, where I took a trip through the Caucasus Mountain ranges that engulf the country. Whilst there, I learnt of the number of ancient groups of Georgian people who have inhabited these mountain ranges for millennia and continue to uphold an array of cultural customs and traditions that have been passed down for generations. Experiencing the remoteness of these environments and how people live within them was very thought-provoking. On the one hand, life in such communities clearly presented some significant challenges. As I came to learn, the remote nature of these communities made accessing key supplies along with good healthcare and education, very difficult. Further, this remoteness greatly inhibits prospects for economic development, meaning such communities rely largely on their own produce and surrounding environmental resources to survive. As a result, all members of the community are forced to work very hard to ensure they have adequate food, and be creative with the limited resources they do have to get by. Observing such challenging living conditions would make it easy to be dismissive of what one could learn from life in such settings compared to life in more developed contexts. However, there were clearly elements to the way life was approached there that allowed for some significant lessons. The undertaking of people to selflessly devote their labours towards building up the community, indeed the very notion of community itself in such settings and the resultant close networks people formed with those around them, as well as the diligence people took to engaging in their daily tasks, were all approaches to life we in more urbanised settings could benefit a lot from.

Writing on what truly makes us happy, Zygmunt Bauman states:

> Whatever your cash and credit standing, you won't find in a shopping mall love and friendship, the pleasures of domesticity, the satisfaction that comes from caring for loved ones or helping a neighbour in distress, the self-esteem to be drawn from work well done, gratifying the workmanship instinct' common to us all....[10]

Perhaps the lack of other, more immediate material comforts makes these pleasures take on greater significance in environments such as these remote Georgian communities. Yet wherever it is that we find ourselves living, this focus on community connectedness, along with the intrinsic reward that comes from engaging in the routine tasks of everyday life, can be applied. There's much we can learn from lives shaped by imposed simplicity. That's not to romanticise the hardships that often accompany them, but to recognise that even within cultures of abundance we can choose to simplify our lives, and place greater emphasis on the things that truly matter. Lessons from cultures different to our own, both past and present, can broaden our perspectives and challenge our assumptions on what makes for a good life.

As we move further towards a more globalised, urbanised and capitalist world, it is important that we continually take stock of the cultural environment that surrounds us and remain focused on living out the values and behaviours that truly help us as humans thrive amidst the cultural norms that may distract us from doing so. As modern society continues to evolve rapidly, educating future generations of people on what behaviours and values are most connected to nurturing good psychological health is an important step forward in helping ease the mental health challenges we are faced with today. By taking a more critical approach to the environment that surrounds us in the twenty-first century and what it tells us will make us happy, we will be better placed to discern the many misleading priorities it presents to us about how we should live. One by one, this process can pave the way for a cultural shift towards a healthier and more flourishing society.

****

Reflecting on the COVID-19 pandemic and the many challenges it presented to everyday life, there exist some enduring lessons that, if implemented throughout our society, could allow for an improvement in our mental health. Firstly, the many hardships the pandemic brought with it serve as a good reminder that we as human beings are all equal. The virus did not discriminate, infecting people regardless of their level of status, bank balance or social media followership. Furthermore, the subsequent restrictions implemented around the world to combat its spread forced many of us to seek out happiness in different ways from those we were accustomed to. For a period of time, we may not have been able to dine at our favourite restaurant or go on a lavish holiday. Instead, people around the world had to make do with largely staying at home, engaging in brief bouts of exercise, and rediscovering hobbies that had perhaps been set aside for some time. Amidst the backdrop of the worldwide chaos the COVID-19 pandemic brought with it, the sense of control many people had over their lives was largely removed, and a life of enforced modesty was given back in return.

Whilst this pandemic was a highly unusual circumstance, its legacy makes a strong case for acknowledging that for too long, our cultural norms were pushing us away from the facets of life that are most important. Whilst far from utopic, in many aspects, life for people today across the developed world has many advantages. Even amidst pandemics, twenty-first century life harbours a range of immense progressions, that enable a greater number of people than ever before to achieve a high standard of living. But now more than ever, it is apparent that with these progressions have come an array of misconceptions around how they should best be utilised in our lives. We have, for example, drawn on the economic advantages available to us to devote our lives towards material gain. We have taken the social freedoms we are today gifted, and somewhat ironically used them to cultivate lifestyles of self-focus and resultant isolation from our communities. And for all the effort put in towards the pursuit of happiness, we often have come to do so with a misunderstanding of how to truly achieve it. These cultural underpinnings, which in part represent humanity's great progress, have come to manifest in ways whereby they also possess the capability to regress it. Living and behaving in ways contrary to the cultural norms that shape our lives is by no means an easy task. But by better understanding what behaviours and lifestyle factors are most likely going to foster positive psychological health outcomes, we can channel our time, energies and attention towards these means to make a difference in our own lives, as well as others as a result.

Chapter 8

The Examined Life

> 'When you arise in the morning, give thanks for the food and for the joy of living. If you see no reason for giving thanks, the fault lies only in yourself.'
> Chief Tecumseh

A good reminder for me that Christmas time is around the corner comes from catching one of the many television screenings of the classic American Christmas-themed film *It's a Wonderful Life*. Released to cinemas in 1946 and frequently cited amidst critics' lists of 'greatest films ever made', its story focuses on the life of a middle-aged bank manager named George. George is shown throughout the film to be a man of good character, devoted to his children, the banking business he inherited from his father, and his small community hometown of Bedford Falls. Despite the many good things in his life, George feels unfulfilled, believing his life hasn't gone to plan. On Christmas Eve, this feeling deepens when a financial calamity strikes his banking business after one of his employees misplaces a large sum of money en route to depositing it into the bank. Completely overwhelmed at the prospect of facing bankruptcy and personal ruin, George walks to the town's bridge where he contemplates jumping. There, he is stopped by an angel named Clarence. When George despondently shares with Clarence that he wishes he had never been born, his request is granted, and he is shown a version of life in his hometown without him ever having existed in it. George is astounded to see his many friends appear different, and in many cases despondent, with their lives having taken lesser paths without his influence. Uncomfortable with what he sees before him, George desperately pleads with the angel to have his life restored. Again, his wish is granted, leading George to gratefully rush home to spend Christmas Eve with his family. Meanwhile, knowing of his financial difficulties, his wife has sought financial support from the community to cover the money that was earlier misplaced. Upon arriving home, George is greeted by his family and friends, and is presented with the money he needs to save both himself and his business. Overwhelmed by their generosity and love, George comes to realise that in spite of all the imperfections of his life, he truly has so much to be thankful for.

With the Christmas period for many a time that allows a brief reprieve from the busyness of normal life and provides a time for reflection, the annual promotion of this film during the festive season is indeed timely. Its message of encouraging us to reflect and be thankful for the truly important things in life in spite of the challenges we may be facing, is perhaps better absorbed and appreciated at a time when we are not as consumed by the pressures of everyday life. The love of family and friends, good health, access to food and water. These are all things we shouldn't need some sort of existential crisis to stop and fully appreciate. That said, it is often only when presented with difficult circumstances that we truly reflect and be thankful for the many good things we have all around us at any given time.

The practice of actively expressing gratitude in our lives has emerged as a powerful psychological tool over the past few decades, with a myriad of research findings indicating that expressing feelings of gratitude, thankfulness, and appreciation is associated with a range of positive wellbeing outcomes. Some of these include the fostering of positive emotions, greater resilience and an improved overall sense of psychological health.[1] This is a connection that has been understood within different religious faiths for centuries, with the cultivation of thankfulness a key virtue embedded within Christian, Jewish, Islamic and Buddhist beliefs. It was only at the beginning of the twenty-first century, however, that the concept of gratitude was increasingly looked at through a scientific lens as a potential clinical tool to improve people's psychological health.

One early study exploring the role gratitude may have on wellbeing was conducted by US Psychologists Robert Emmons and Michael McCullough.[2] Here, the researchers ran an experiment whereby participants were placed into one of three different groups. The first of these groups was required to write a daily journal about all the negative events or hassles in their life, the second group were asked to write daily about the things for which they were grateful in their life, and the third group simply wrote about neutral life events, with all groups also simultaneously completing a survey that measured their psychological wellbeing. Across the various study conditions, the group focused on writing about the things they were grateful for consistently showed higher wellbeing scores in comparison with the other two study groups, as well as greater levels of optimism and life satisfaction. A wealth of subsequent research has since replicated these findings, showing practising expressions of gratitude is associated with not just positive psychological health outcomes, but improved physical health, more fulfilling personal relationships and increased work satisfaction.[3]

Engaging in tasks such as writing a gratitude diary and reflecting on a few key things you may be thankful for on any given day is a proven and practical way of fostering feelings of thankfulness and in turn bolstering our psychological state. As well as assisting with our immediate psychological state, practising gratitude on a daily basis can help cultivate an enduring 'lifestyle' of gratitude, whereby brief moments of feeling grateful merge into a mindset of being persistently aware of all that is good around us. This is not a mindset of ignorance whereby we may ignore the things that are going wrong in either our own lives or the world around us, but instead centres on focusing our attention on the good things that may be present in our lives at any given time, irrespective of what challenges we may be facing. Within this process, we may also come to apply a different perspective to a challenging situation we are facing. As an example of this, towards the end of the University semester, when assignment deadlines begin looming, I often encourage the students I am teaching that amidst all the stress and pressure they are currently facing, it is worth remembering that they once upon a time likely desired to be exactly where they were at that moment. That is, enrolled in the course of study that they perhaps once proudly celebrated being admitted to and working towards their desired career. For all the stressors these students may be dealing with at this time, working through these hurdles was going to get them closer towards the completion of their degrees and towards hopefully obtaining a job they were interested in. An outcome that is no small thing. Such a perspective shift does not necessarily alleviate the stress of this heightened workload they are facing, nor the pressures they may feel to obtain certain grades, but it does put this stress into perspective and allow for a more reflective approach to the situation at hand. Essentially, by making a consistent 'choice' to have an attitude of appreciation for the good that is around us, and not just occasionally thinking about these things, we can cultivate a mindset of thankfulness. This is an outlook we can foster and grow by practice. Life is of course inevitably going to present us with challenging times, as well as daily stress-inducing situations, but maintaining a perspective of gratitude can allow us to see past these challenges and remain focused on the good.

The founder of Positive Psychology, Martin Seligman, describes a process similar to this, which he calls 'learned optimism'.[4] According to Seligman, learned optimism involves an outlook whereby people can consciously learn to cultivate their thoughts towards a more optimistic disposition, with thoughts of gratitude a core accomplice to this. To unpack this idea further, take for instance this example of a story I once heard a teacher share of two builders working alongside each other on a building site that was to become a new school. I am paraphrasing based on memory, but the teacher shared that the first of the two builders marched into work feeling disgruntled and unenthusiastic about the day ahead, knowing how tiresome and laborious the work ahead of him was to be on this particular day. This builder spent the day lamenting the demanding and thankless nature of his job and would regularly check his watch in immense anticipation of finishing time. Alongside him worked another builder, one who arrived at work enthusiastic and eager. He carried an excitement towards the project at hand, one whereby he saw himself as contributing to building a space where future generations of children were going to come to learn, grow, and laugh. Despite the physically challenging nature of the task, he saw it as an amazing opportunity to stay in shape and relish being in the outdoors. Further, the enormity of the task ahead meant secure and ongoing work that would allow him to earn an income sufficient to help care for his family, a reality he was very thankful for. Here, we see an example of two people in the very same situation, perceiving their place in it very differently. If we are truly honest with ourselves, we are all likely to have had days when we feel like the first builder, weary and unmotivated. However, the example of the second builder provides us with an illustration of the role perspective can play in shaping our reality, and specifically, the power a mindset of focusing on whatever good may surround our situation can have in enhancing our daily experiences and quality of life.

A Mindset of 'More'

Beyond the inevitable difficulties of life, one of the challenges presented to us in fostering an enduring perspective of gratitude in the modern world exists in the many messages that surround us, informing us that we need 'more'. Living in a consumption-oriented society, we are constantly encouraged to strive for 'more'. 'Own more stuff', 'achieve more', 'become more'. Such messages and the resultant cognition they foster can lead us to consequently place our attention on what we may lack in life — both the tangible and intangible — and away from contentment and gratitude for what we already have. Throughout human history, the vast majority of people have aspired to the love of family and friends, good health, adequate food and water supplies, shelter, and safety from harm. Across the developed world today, we generally view these things as a given — the baseline of a good life — often expecting to have everything else thrown in as well. This may include driving a nice car, acquiring a certain level of status within our community, and fostering a particular type of lifestyle that we may find alluring. Whilst there is nothing at all wrong with desiring these things, as we have explored in previous chapters, issues begin to arise when we overstate their importance in our lives and allow them to overshadow our more fundamental innate needs. The pursuit of this modern privilege can leave people stretched in both time and finances in ways not conducive to a balanced life. This can manifest by way of forcing ourselves to work harder, spend less time with our loved ones, and oftentimes internalising our focus on ourselves (and away from broader societal concerns) in order to keep up with these lifestyle demands we feel we need to achieve. Furthermore, as previously touched on, often when we reach these desires, whilst we may feel satisfied for a period of time, if we don't practice being content with what we have around us, any feelings of satisfaction we experience can be time-limited. A wonderful allegory about the consequences of constantly desiring more exists in the classic Russian fairy tale: *The Tale of the Fisherman and the Fish*. Written in the early nineteenth century by Alexander Pushkin, the story tells of an elderly fisherman and his wife who live in a small hut by the seaside. One day as the fisherman is out fishing in the nearby sea, he catches a 'golden fish', who shocks the old man by verbally asking to be returned to the sea, promising the fisherman any wish in return: 'Put me back, old man, into the ocean — I will pay you a right royal ransom, I will give you whatever you ask me'. The fisherman, understandably startled by the fish and its ability to speak, agrees to its request and humbly shares that he does not need anything in return. Returning home, he excitedly recalls his experiences to his wife, who responds to his enthusiasm with not awe nor curiosity, but frustration, harshly demanding that he goes back to find the fish and wish for a new washtub to replace their broken one. So, the old man returns to the scene of his meeting with the fish, who again appears, and is happy to grant this request for a new washtub. True to his word, upon returning home the old man is greeted with a new washtub sitting outside his hut. Any expectations that this would appease his wife, however, are quickly dashed, with her again harshly rebuking him: 'Oh you simpleton! Oh you great silly! To ask for a tub — a mere washtub! What good can you get from a washtub? Return to the goldfish, you silly, bow down low and ask for a cottage'. The old man again yields to her request, as does the fish, with the man this time returning home to find a cottage standing in the place of their former hut. Satisfaction is not granted there however, with the old man journeying back and forth between his wife and the fish, with her ever-increasing demands to next become a noble lady, then ruler of the province, the Tsaritsa, and then finally the ruler of all of the sea, with the golden fish as her faithful servant. Upon returning to the seashore to make what would be his final request, the fish hears the old man's appeal for his wife to be made ruler of the sea, however, this time does not respond, and instead silently swims off into the distance. The fable concludes with the old man returning home, where he is greeted with his original mud hut, complete with a broken washtub sitting out the front.

The message of this famous fable is clear and simple. It highlights the pitfalls of greed and the importance of being grateful for what we already have right now, no matter how little or much. Reading this story, I am compelled to think of the fisherman's wife as a metaphor for that voice in our own minds that is ever critiquing our circumstances and constantly demanding 'more'. It is of course natural to want to improve on our life's circumstances and to ever be striving to be better. This may particularly be the case if we find ourselves living in similar undesirable conditions to those the fisherman and his wife were enduring. But provided we are in good health and have adequate living conditions and resources, our aspirations for more don't have to lead us into being dismissive and discontented with our present situation. We can, of course, be content and thankful for our present circumstances, even whilst pursuing bigger and better things in our lives. Today's environment of social media, mass advertising and the culture of instant gratification that surrounds us, can present challenges to us living in contentment. However, we can still pursue our goals for the future while simultaneously being thankful for where we are right now and with whatever good may come to us on any given day. Perhaps it's simply that one stranger who smiled at us earlier, maybe it's a clear blue sky or an enjoyable meal you were able to share with friends. As challenging as life can be, there are indeed good things all around us if we are willing to look outside of the problems we may be facing, and challenge these with a greater focus on the positives in our lives.

A Matter of Perspective

Recently, I spent some time in Moldova, a small nation nestled between Ukraine and Romania. Whilst there, I had the privilege of helping out at an aid organisation based in the country's west, which at the time was running its annual 'summer camps' for young people who lived in the region. In this particular year, these camps were more crowded than usual due to the horrific war that had broken out only months earlier in neighbouring Ukraine. The war had led to millions of Ukrainian families seeking refuge from their homeland, with many fleeing into neighbouring Moldova to do so. This organisation was subsequently able to use its facilities to provide accommodation and meals to a number of these families who were in need. By the time I arrived, some of these families — made up largely of mothers and their children (males between 18 and 60 years of age were not permitted to leave Ukraine at this time, meaning many a husband and father was left behind to help with the war effort) — had already been at this facility for months, living with just a scant few of their possessions and clothes. As well as their possessions, they had left behind their entire lives back in their cities or villages that they had been forced to abandon, including their jobs, their network of friends and their children's schools. Despite this, as well as the unimaginable horrors many had endured after Russia's full-scale invasion of their homeland commenced, every morning they would diligently attend the village's daily chapel service, and the children would then bound out full of energy and enthusiastically and joyfully engage in the games that the camp ran for them throughout the day. I was asked constantly to join in for soccer, basketball and volleyball games, motivated to do so by the infectious enthusiasm with which they were played. Speaking with these families interchangeably between my non-fluent Ukrainian and their non-fluent English, I came to learn of some of the unimaginable horrors that they had experienced as a result of the war and the subsequent disorder and chaos it had meant for their lives. Unsurprisingly, most families expressed a strong desire to return home as soon as it was safe to do so, or failing that, hoped to seek refuge in Western Europe. In the meantime, they were grateful for the safety they had been given at this organisation. Of course, there were severe feelings of grief, stress and uncertainty that these people were dealing with. Yet instead of focussing on these immense hardships, as well as the daily happenings of the horrible conflict taking place in their homeland just miles away, they were fully present to the fact they had come to a place of safety, where they had shelter and food available to them. A reality many Ukrainians had tragically been deprived of at this time. For all the stressors, uncertainty and recent trauma these people were experiencing, they were choosing to focus their perspective on the positives of their situation and look forward with a profound outlook of hope. One of the amazing gifts these Ukrainians gave me through the time I spent with them was the understanding that even amidst the most challenging of times, we can choose to frame our own outlook in either a positive or a negative fashion. Indeed, as illustrated in the fable of the old man and the golden fish, even amidst abundance, we can have a perspective of lack and an unquenchable yearning for more. Such an illusion seems especially pronounced in wealthy societies, whereby people so often compare themselves to their peers and are consequently so prone to an endless psyche of desiring 'more'. Despite the relative affluence afforded to people within wealthy, politically stable and conflict-free environments, so often our outlook is one whereby we focus on what we may lack rather than the abundance we have all around us.

This is a notion that became further embedded within me across a number of later visits I made to Ukraine during the time of this horrible war. One of these visits held the purpose of conducting interviews with young people for a research project I was working on, exploring the many ways the war had impacted their everyday lives as well as their mental health. Almost unanimously, the young people I was fortunate enough to spend time with across my visits talked of the way in which the war had fostered within them a newfound appreciation for life. This was initially a very difficult notion for me to grasp: how could one better appreciate life amidst the atrocities they were being forced to live through every single day? I thought. Yet the more time I spent in the country and the more people I met whilst there, the more this idea began to make sense to me. Consistently, these amazingly resilient young people expressed how this horrible environment of war had compelled them to live a life whereby they made every moment count, actively seeking to make the most of every day of life they were given, and doing so no longer bound to the more trivial worries of everyday life. This, they expressed, was not an approach of negligence that saw them ignore the impact of the danger, devastation and tragedy that was all around them. Instead, they shared that being surrounded by such terror and sadness had allowed them to focus attentively on what truly matters and no longer worry about the smaller concerns of life as they had done previously. One young man I met with who had recently returned from a period of time serving on the front lines shared this with particular clarity. This young soldier shared that since the beginning of the war, the comparatively minor worries of day-to-day life no longer bothered him. In his words, he came to the realisation that life is too short to worry. Faced with living in a warzone, the prospect of death he shared became a very real one, and it was within this context that he came to form a far greater appreciation of life. Based on the horrifying experiences he had endured serving on the front lines, he also shared the way these experiences had fostered a newfound appreciation for the 'normal life' he had lived before the war commenced. This appreciation, he elaborated, applied to the job he used to work, the normal activities he got to engage in on any given day, and the people he got to spend time with away from the challenges of war. Essentially, he shared the ways in which the war had led to a profound shift in his perspective about what was most important and the fact that life should not be taken for granted. This is an outlook that it shouldn't take living amidst a warzone for us to be reminded of. He went on to elaborate that this newfound approach to his life was not an ethos of no longer caring about anything, nor partying the remainder of his youth away. It was more about simply not giving time to worry about things that are not as important as we can so easily make them out to be in our minds and instead focusing on what is, such as one's health, relationships and dreams. I was deeply impacted by these sentiments and perspectives that were very much a theme of the conversations I had with other young people also right across the country. Again, it shouldn't take living amidst a warzone to implement what one young person I spoke with termed the 'Ukrainian mindset', an outlook of embracing every day of life and focussing on what really matters. We can value the important things in our lives while neglecting the worries that really don't mean that much right now.

There are of course many unique challenges modern environments present to us that may hamper our propensity towards a mindset of appreciation and gratitude that should not be dismissed. Nor should these challenges be trivialised because there are people in other parts of the world faring much worse than we might be. Indeed, beyond the inevitable trials of life, such as those to do with our relationships, health or grief, modern life also presents us with challenges specific to the technologically driven, fast-paced lives we often lead today that can in turn present serious stressors to our lives. These challenges can stem from the fluctuating economies, unstable job markets and the ever-increasing costs of living that surround us, as just a few of the issues that can justly consume our attention and in turn can make the prospect of living a life of gratitude particularly difficult. It should be noted here also, that even amidst wealthy countries, issues such as poverty still abound. As of 2021, just over ten per cent of US people live below the poverty line, with a similar percentage figure seen in

Australia, Canada and Germany.[5] It is likely in all of these nations that a much larger percentage of people would also live in a way whereby they seriously struggle to make ends meet. For the remaining population, despite these social and economic challenges consistent with modern life that can lead us to feel overwhelmed and anxious, a visit to the many impoverished or conflict-riddled regions of the world would likely lead to a prompt reassessment of our present circumstances. Further, the trials we face today are often incomparable to those experienced by our ancestors, who often lived in circumstances of extreme poverty, oppression and injustice when compared to today. It is indeed true that even amidst pandemics, global instability, and political and economic uncertainty, across the developed world today we enjoy significantly higher standards of living than ever before. Perhaps the next time you are feeling frustrated or worried by an issue that is not life-threatening, it is worth reminding yourself of the reality that if you live in a context free from warfare, have a roof over your head and can afford to eat three meals a day, then you have won what philosophers term the 'lottery of birth'. The lottery of birth is the name given to a philosophical argument originally proposed by Enlightenment thinkers such as John Locke and Jean Jacques Rousseau, which essentially theorises that since we are unable to choose the circumstances into which we are born, we should not be held responsible for them. Political philosopher John Rawls explores this notion within his 'veil of ignorance theory'.[6] Here, Rawls suggests that since we do not know whether we are to be born into resource-rich conditions or resource-poor contexts, it is important we act to ensure that everyone has the same rights and opportunities. As well as encouraging us to utilise the resources we have to lift others up, this framework is also highly provocative towards how we think about our own place in the world and the significant gratitude we should feel if we were born into a context whereby we have the sufficient resources, security, and freedoms to live a thriving life. The probability of being born at a time and a place whereby this is so would be so marginal that it would be almost negligible.

To reiterate, we today still face very real challenges and issues consistent with the human experience throughout history, including health-related concerns, lived experiences of trauma and grief, financial pressures, political unease and relationship breakdowns. Further, we live in a time plagued by economic and environmental uncertainty, whereby the global financial markets we have come to rely on seem increasingly volatile, and more significantly, the future of the very planet we live on is challenged. Undoubtedly, these issues present grave concerns and stressors that can justifiably lead to us experiencing adverse psychological responses. Interestingly, though, according to a survey conducted by the American Psychological Association, American peoples' worries today centre primarily around work stresses and financial pressures.[7] These findings are mirrored by similar surveys that have been conducted in other developed nations that also show finances and work-related stresses, as well as family conflicts and — believe it or not — 'keeping up with social media' as people's most significant causes of stress.[8] Relatively speaking, most of these issues present as very real threats that can understandably lead to high levels of stress, anxiety and even trauma. They therefore should not be taken lightly. However, as difficult and demanding as life can be today, it is again worth reminding ourselves of the impact these challenges we face have on our lives today compared to the challenges of days gone by. For instance, as taxing as it can be working long hours in a job we may find challenging, to be employed in a role whereby we are provided with a fair level of remuneration and personal rights is a privilege many before us never experienced, nor do many others across the globe today. Further, whilst our planet's future and the consequences of human destruction absolutely need to be acted upon, we today have the scientific understanding and resources necessary to take the appropriate steps to curb this impact. With environmental concerns in days gone by, such as severe winters, drought and natural disasters, far more difficult to predict and address. Modern life is undoubtedly hard in its own unique way, presenting us with new challenges distinct to the economic and technologically driven world we live in. However, referring back to Rawls' lottery of birth thesis, given such a choice, I would still choose to live in an environment whereby, in spite of these difficulties, my access to food, water and shelter, as well as my basic level of safety, is exorbitantly higher than any other time in history. A reality that should not be taken for granted. Whatever the challenges we may be facing, we are indeed fortunate to live at a time whereby our survival is likely not dependent on the quality of the next harvest of the village we live in, nor are our thoughts consumed by the constant threat of warfare that once defined life for much of the world.

It is also worth considering here that these poverties and injustices that plagued the world in centuries gone by are still very much a reality for people living across the globe today. According to a report from the World Bank Database, 736 million people (as of October 2021) live in extreme poverty, surviving on less than $1.90US per day.[9] Over 10 per cent of the world's population still relies on untreated surface water as their drinking water, and roughly 6.2 million children die of preventable malnourishment every year.[10] These are confronting statistics. However, along with compelling us to respond to the needs of others, such figures should provide us with a strong perspective specific to some of our own worries and anxieties. Life outside of such challenging circumstances may be far from perfect, with corruption, crime, social inequalities, economic and environmental concerns, and health issues still everyday threats to people's lives. Furthermore, intense grief, hardship and suffering are inescapable parts of the human experience, irrespective of one's social context. However, in spite of these challenges, if we again live in an environment where we are blessed with a level of security, freedom and the means to feed and house ourselves, we should be immensely grateful for the prosperity and comforts we enjoy. These are privileges that we can too easily miss amidst our busy lives.

I remember travelling through South-East Asia in my mid-twenties and, for the first time, being exposed to a slum in Thailand. Through this experience I received a strong dose of perspective in relation to the life I was living back home in Melbourne, Australia. Seeing children desperately begging for food, large families living in tiny and dilapidated living quarters and learning about the harsh realities for people living in such impoverished regions left me to seriously contemplate the comparative privileges of my life. To be frank, it left me with a sense of shame towards some of the attitudes I had carried about my own existence. These included the resentment I at times felt towards my perceived lack of finances, towards the bitter inner dialogue I sometimes engaged with around not having achieved what I would have liked to in some areas of my life, and the complete apathy I often felt for the many material and security comforts I had in place around me. This reflection was not to say I, like most people, had not been through hardships that should be disregarded, nor that I did not have a range of immediate challenges that were in front of me. Rather, it was to suggest that whilst life can be hard, there was much that I should have been more focussed on and grateful for, and instead of being preoccupied with my own worries, there were others around the world facing significantly greater troubles than I that I should have been far more concerned about.

My experience is by no means unique, with witnessing firsthand the hardships embedded in disadvantaged environments often providing people with an opportunity to alter their perspectives. I would also argue that my subsequent response of all too soon moving past this perspective shift and re-engaging with the desires and allures of modern life upon my return home would be a common one for others also. Integrating these perspective shifts presents an opportunity to act, and in doing so, to become increasingly aware and grateful for our own situation and the many resources we often take for granted. Finding a way to stay engaged with helping people in need beyond such experiences, be it through regularly donating to a charity or even volunteering time to your own local community, are all positive actions that can help not only serve the needs of others, but also help maintain a sense of perspective about our own lives. Thinking locally, there is undoubtedly a range of unmet needs and instances of relative poverty or ill health within the community you live in that would significantly benefit from your contributions. These localised needs prove that charity starts at home and that a trip to a different cultural context is not necessary to instil a perspective change. Right now, in any major city around the world, there are homeless people sleeping out in the cold, single parents struggling to raise their children on their own and understaffed hospitals that are crying out for the help of volunteers. Choosing to offer some time towards these means will not only provide valuable help to those that need it, but it may also help you gain a perspective that is outside of yourself and allow a firmer appreciation for all that you do have (and stop focussing on whatever it is that you may not). Irrespective of the constant challenges we face as both individuals and as a society today, life with a roof over your head, adequate food and water, as well as stable levels of security and freedom, puts us in an enviable position compared to many others. It is well worth remembering this as we go about our day-to-day lives, as well as our daily decisions around how we choose to live them. We should not take any of the good things in our world for granted, but rather allow them to feed our disposition of gratitude and want to help others.

****

The idea of seeing our life through the lens of an alternate world in which we never existed, as presented in *It's a Wonderful Life*, is a very interesting thought experiment. I wonder what good things you may have missed over the years while you were preoccupied with work-related stressors, keeping up with the latest trends on social media, or desperately holding out on your next big purchase? Much like George came to discover throughout the film, for all of the trials and unfulfilled wants we may have in our lives. There are likely good things happening all around us that we aren't paying enough attention to. A disposition of thankfulness and good fortune does not need to be exclusive to one or the other. In fact, learning to find things to be grateful for amidst hardship is a proven method of providing the resilience and strength necessary to see through difficult times. On the other hand, as detailed in the story of the old man and the goldfish, we can be gifted with everything we ever wanted and still want more. Leaving us dissatisfied and ungrateful for all we may lack, rather than content with all we do have. Essentially, fostering feelings of gratitude is not about circumstance; it is about choice.

Carrying a perspective of gratitude towards the likely many good things we already have in our lives, circumstances we often today take for granted can act as an effective way to calm our desires for more while also awakening us to the immense resources we have to contribute to the lives of those around us. It is difficult to be truly grateful for all the good things we do have and simultaneously be self-focussed and entirely bogged down by concerns to do with ourselves. American poet and civil-rights activist Maya Angelou shared the following in relation to gratitude in her own life:

> The ship of my life may or may not be sailing on calm and amiable seas. The challenging days of my existence may or may not be bright and promising. Stormy or sunny days, glorious or lonely nights, I maintain an attitude of gratitude. If I insist on being pessimistic, there is always tomorrow. Today, I am blessed.

Whatever the circumstances we are facing, choosing to be grateful for even the smallest of things can allow us a sense of peace amidst the chaos that may be all around us.

Cultural Deceptions: How progress is making us miserable and how we can get back on track

Chapter 9

A Good Life is a Meaningful Life

> 'What man actually needs is not a tensionless state but rather the striving and struggling for some goal worthy of him.'
> Victor Frankl

One of the more unique places I have ever visited is the now relatively small township of Moynoq, located in the Republic of Karakalpakstan in Western Uzbekistan. Moynoq could be best described as a fishing village with a difference. I had long been intrigued by this particular town, as not so long ago if you had looked at its location on a map, you would have found a township located on the banks of a large inland body of water known as the Aral Sea. Indeed, throughout most of its history, this was the case, with Moynoq once a fishing haven as well as a popular waterside tourist spot for Uzbeks to escape the summer heat. This all began to change in the 1970s however, when Uzbekistan, then under Soviet rule, was earmarked by the leadership of the Soviet Union to become the largest cotton-producing region in the world. The issue with this intention, however, was that the regions that had been designated for cotton farming were mainly desert. So, in order to get sufficient water to cater for the many new cotton fields that were being established, the decision was made by authorities in Moscow that the two rivers that served the Aral Sea would be diverted away from it and instead directed towards these new cotton fields. Despite repeated warnings from scientists against this decision due to the disastrous consequences it could have for the health of the Aral Sea, the rivers were diverted. Sure enough, over the coming decades, the Aral Sea would slowly but surely dry up, existing today at just five per cent of its original size. For the township of Moynoq, the consequences of this catastrophic environmental decision made all those years ago are a town that is today built around a dry port, complete with a number of piers that stretch out over the sand, a 'graveyard' of ships that have been left to rot away in the now desert, and an eco-system that has been thrown into disarray, with summer temperatures frequently exceeding fifty-degrees celsius, and wild dust storms regularly sweep across the now barren plains of the former seabed.

Away from the stark environmental disaster that has taken place here, equally tragic is the plight of the people who have been left behind without their sea, as well as often their livelihoods that were based around it. During my time in Moynoq, I was introduced through my guide to a number of people who had grown up in the region, who shared their stories of once having worked on the waters on fishing boats or in the town's now abandoned fish factory. By the late 1980s however, the body of water that surrounded their village had receded rapidly. The townsfolk were forced to drive upwards of an hour to get to an appropriate fishing spot. After a number of years, with the sea receding even further, this drive became untenable, leaving people unable to fish, the fish factory no longer operable, and a good portion of the town's population were left without a living. Walking the streets of Moynoq, there was an obvious sense of loss amongst those who had remained in this once thriving seaside town. While some people are undertaking significant work to rebuild their community and ensure

Moynoq and its surroundings are a better environment for the next generation of its inhabitants, this sense of loss was still clearly expressed in a number of ways. The many abandoned fish factories visible throughout the town, the boarded-up houses, and, more personally, the downcast expressions many people seemed to carry on their faces. Walking the streets of this town, there was an almost tangible feeling of grief over the loss of their sea and a resultant pessimism about the region's future prospects. This sense of gloom was further expressed through the stories relayed to me of the locals still living there, people who perhaps were once fishermen, seafarers, tourist operators or just lovers of water, who now sat idly around in the extreme heat. Through no fault of their own, they were left without their livelihoods, as well as the once beautiful seascape that surrounded their township. Tragically, people live amidst similar disheartening circumstances all around the world, with this particularly so in contexts whereby employment prospects are limited, and again through no fault of their own, people find themselves lacking a sense of vocation and purpose. Away from the dire financial challenges this presents to people, without a day-to-day sense of purpose, our sense of self-worth diminishes, and often with it, so too does our emotional state.

Living in a developed, urbanised environment, the prospects for employment are of course significantly greater than in an environment without a developed industry and infrastructure sector. If you were to stand in the middle of any major city across the capitalist world within business hours, you would likely observe a scene of people busily rushing around from one place to the next with a seemingly deliberate sense of purpose in their stride. It goes without saying that life looks very different in a big city environment than it is in the small Uzbeki village of Moynoq. Scenes such as those displayed across the bustling cities of the world outwardly portray the image of a purpose-driven people, although this image can be deceptive. For all the busyness and fast-paced nature of modern life for those fortunate enough to be employed across such environments, if those energies aren't channelled towards some sort of fulfilling end goal, people can feel just as unfulfilled as they may in a small village with limited employment prospects. In spite of the increased opportunities and resources available to people across the developed world today, as we will explore throughout this chapter, without a true and abiding sense of meaning in their lives, people can still report feeling a sense of futility and hopelessness in these opportunity-rich contexts.[1] Truly understanding the significant opportunities and resources available to us today leads to the final, and perhaps most significant principle necessary in better navigating the complexities of modern life and the culture that shapes it. That of pursuing a life of meaning and purpose that extends beyond oneself.

Factors that Constitute Meaning in Life

Psychological research defines meaning in life as the extent to which people comprehend and understand their life experiences, as well as the drive and motivation they have towards an overarching life purpose and mission.[2] One's perception of meaning in life therefore, captures their capacity to make sense of their life, pursue some sort of end purpose, and lead a life that is ultimately worthwhile and significant. Wellbeing theorists suggest cultivating a life of 'meaning' along these lines is actually a core component of fostering good wellbeing, and a fundamental cornerstone of a flourishing life.[3] It should come as no surprise then, that a wealth of scientific studies have shown people who report greater meaning in their lives experience better wellbeing outcomes, both psychologically and physically, along with higher levels of optimism, hope and better relationships with others.[4]

Victor Frankl writes that a strong sense of life meaning provides for a clear vision of one's future, a sense of existential purpose and satisfaction, and in turn, relates profoundly to life satisfaction and fulfilment.[5] Frankl adds that when a true sense of meaning in life is lacking, a person is prone to experiencing feelings of hopelessness, the perception that they lack control over their life, and the absence of any true abiding personal objectives. Further psychological research has associated a sense of meaning in life with greater resilience and acceptance of adversity, highlighting its role as an important protective factor against the effects of negative life events.[6] During the COVID-19 pandemic, for example, I along with my co-researcher Olivia Vari were interested in exploring how a self-perceived meaning in life may help safeguard against some of the stressors and worries brought about by the pandemic.[7] Based on survey responses collected in the midst of the pandemic's lockdown period that began in March of 2020, our findings showed that those who reported a higher meaning in life also reported feeling less stressed and worried specific to the various threats related to COVID-19.

With the significant progresses in health care, education and technology, as well as the increased economic and social developments afforded to us today, the opportunity we have today to pursue a life that is truly meaningful to us is greater than ever before. This truth, however, can very easily be clouded by the many demands of modern life in these contexts. Perhaps it's the overdue bills we are struggling to pay, the particularly busy time we are experiencing at our place of work or the unexpected medical costs we have just been greeted with. Further, in the context of a globalised world full of problems that seem well beyond our reach, beginning to apply our efforts towards making a difference on a social or environmental platform can seem completely overwhelming. These realities of modern life can make a compelling case for us to turn our thinking back towards ourselves, at best seeking to fulfil our own self-interests, and at worst just doing what we need to do to get by. But these challenges shouldn't blind us from the needs of those around us and the unique aptitudes we each have to be able to make a difference towards helping meet the needs of others.

With that said, the many demands we are faced with today that may distract us from taking action towards making a positive contribution to the world around us can, on the other hand, demonstrate the very truth that the opportunity we have to make an impact on the world is indeed greater today than ever before. For instance, have you ever considered when you you reluctantly go to pay your electricity bill what a privilege it is to live in an environment that so freely offers electrical power when there are millions of people around the world right now who are forced to live largely without it? Similarly, the next time you find yourself tired and perhaps frustrated by your long commute home from work, it is worth remembering that there are people all around the world currently afflicted by conflict, poverty or political instability who would love to be in your position right now — safely returning home after a full day of being employed.

Despite the many advantages that come with living in developed settings today, some research findings suggest that people living in high-income countries are less inclined to feel a strong sense of purpose and meaning in their lives than people living in lower-income nations. Drawing on data from a large international data set that included questions assessing one's sense of meaning in life, cross-cultural psychologists Shigehiro Oishi and Ed Diener found that people living in lower-income countries reported feeling a stronger sense of meaning in life than those in wealthier countries.[8] These findings seem somewhat contradictory when we reflect on the many challenges people often face in lower-income environments and, in particular, the reduced opportunities and resources people may have at their disposal to pursue their aspirations compared to people living in higher-income contexts. In response to these findings, the authors put forward a few possible explanations as to why a sense of life meaning may differ so much between poorer and wealthier cultures. These include, firstly, the significant role religion often plays in poorer nations versus wealthier nations as a symbol of life's meaning and purpose. Further, the preoccupation with survival people in low-income countries can face is noted as another possible explanation, with this for some day-to-day struggle to provide adequate food and security to one's family likely providing a clear sense of life meaning in and of itself. Most compellingly, however, the researchers also theorise that people are more likely to construct meaning from difficult life circumstances than through comfortable ones. That is to say, when people are confronted with challenging events or situations, they may construct a deep sense of meaning out of that very instance. Be it injustice, suffering or hardship, revolving around trying to rectify the situation. While on the surface, this may make a degree of sense, this idea presents a challenge to the developed world, as well as how we take for granted the many comforts and securities provided within it. These comforts may well be responsible for limiting the scope of what people living in circumstances of relative prosperity choose to aspire to, both individually and collectively, to merely desiring to achieve a life of security and financial comfort.

In many respects, it makes sense for people today who are fortunate enough to be employed amidst an economically stable environment to adopt a 'play it safe approach' specific to the objectives they have for their lives. Secure as good a paying job as possible, use the income from that job to pay the rent or mortgage, perhaps raise a family, and in the process try to experience as much happiness as possible. These are great aims and objectives that are, in the main, highly fulfilling in and of themselves. Yet, we shouldn't let the pursuit of such things consume our attention in a way whereby we come to focus too greatly on ourselves and in turn they distract us from the needs of our community. Once upon a time, people were forced into a sense of selflessness and mutual cooperation as a means of survival. If we reflect on life in medieval Britain for example, significant work would take place across the spring and summer months to ensure sufficient grain and other food supplies were harvested to provide townsfolk with adequate sustenance throughout the region's long and dreary winters. At such a time, people were often engaged with tasks within their community that went beyond their everyday employment, such as assisting with these harvesting efforts, or with helping to secure their village from the very real threat of attack from neighbouring powers. Today, across the developed world, we are fortunate not to be faced with the task of ensuring our impending food security nor to employ such a collective effort to ensure the survival of our community. Indeed, as we have established, we need not do very much for our community at all if we do not want to. With our goals and aspirations often existing within the realm of the self and centred on achieving personal ambitions ahead of outcomes that might improve the lives of society as a whole.

This is of course not exclusively the case, with brilliant scientists, businesspeople, healthcare workers and teachers, amongst others, doing amazing things to advance the cause of humanity all over the world. Such inclinations towards bettering the planet should not be left to just those we deem to be doing 'extraordinary things', however. It is my belief that everyone has a unique and special purpose they are called to follow in making the world a better place. This may not be as a Nobel Prize-winning scientist or an Olympic athlete, but it may be as one who diligently contributes to their local community and in the process improves the lives of the people that live within it. This is a sense of purpose that may lack some of the glamour of the formerly mentioned vocations, but such a pursuit is absolutely no less important.

The Quest for Meaning

Most people would lay claim to having some sort of sense of meaning on which they base their lives. This may revolve around working a job they feel dedicated to, raising a family, or ticking off items from their 'bucket list'. Indeed, it is of course true that people construct meaning in their lives in many different ways. Psychological research again frequently employs the distinction of *hedonic* as well as *eudaimonic* approaches in establishing the differing paths people take to pursue meaning in their lives. Here, hedonic approaches to meaning refer to those focused on doing so via feelings of happiness, comfort and pleasure. Eudaimonic approaches, on the other hand, focus on the pursuit of complex and meaningful goals as the pathway to meaning in life.[9] Due to its focus on innate psychological needs, research shows that when a person's sense of meaning is framed around eudaimonic aims, they tend to report feeling a stronger sense of personal meaning in their lives.[10] A study conducted by Melissa Grouden and Paul Jose of the University of Wellington, for instance, found that sources of meaning connected to family, interpersonal relations, social issues as well as one's work most closely aligned with a person feeling a stronger sense of meaning in their life, and were also related to a number of positive wellbeing outcomes.[11] Despite these advantages, further research indicates that pursuing a life of meaning via eudaimonic aims over hedonic ones can come at a price. Findings from a number of studies led by eminent social psychologist Roy Baumeister showed that pursuing a life of deep meaningfulness was actually associated with higher levels of worry, stress, and anxiety when compared to pursuing outcomes of 'comfort' and 'happiness'.[12] Here, the researchers found that satisfying one's immediate needs and wants increased their happiness, but was largely irrelevant to any feelings of meaningfulness. Pursuing happiness was also linked with lower levels of worry than meaningfulness. However, it was also linked with more selfish attitudes and behaviours when compared with those who reported high levels of life meaning and who also reported a stronger desire to give to those in need and make a positive contribution to society. Thinking about the earlier chapter exploring Western notions of happiness, a sense of life meaning centred on 'eudaimonic' pursuits allows us to go beyond pursuits of comfort and in-the-moment happiness. At times this can of course mean sacrificing our personal momentary comfort in exchange for an action that may very well be seen at the time as uncomfortable. A good analogy of this is the act of making a choice to leave the comfort of your loungeroom couch to go and engage in some physical exercise. For many, the in-the-moment feelings experienced whilst exercising may be fatigue, difficulty and discomfort. Feelings that starkly contrast with the feelings of comfort or even perceived happiness one may experience while relaxing on the couch. In the longer term however, the many physical and psychological health benefits that come with engaging in physical activity are well known, making the choice of going for a run over remaining on the couch a positive one. Similarly, when we pursue meaning over pursuing comfort, we may sacrifice pleasurable experiences and moments of comfort to do so. However, the longer-term benefits of pursuing a life centred on helping others and making a contribution to the world around us will likely always outweigh those associated with in-the-moment comfort and happiness.

Establishing a sense of meaning in our lives may seem like a complex, and perhaps even overwhelming task. However, it doesn't have to be. Ask yourself, what skills have you developed across your lifespan, and how could you use these to help others? What resources do you have at your disposal? What unique experiences have you lived through that you may be able to utilise to help others going through the same thing? And what social causes really resonate with you, stirring up within you a desire to see change? These are all questions that can be used as a guide towards facilitating a sense of meaning in your life that extends beyond yourself and contributes to the lives of those around you. It should be said here that responding to these questions and taking action towards fulfilling a sense of meaning in your life doesn't require you to quit your day job so you can dedicate all your time to doing charitable work. For many this is not a realistic option. As mentioned earlier, being employed is a wonderful thing irrespective of how you may feel about your current job. Indeed, for many of us, our job is not the vehicle through which we find our sense of life purpose, but rather a way of making ends meet. If for example, you love sport but were never quite talented enough to make it to the professional ranks, in addition to your day-to-day employment, you may wish to take up a coaching role at a junior sports club and, in the process, develop a sense of meaning around positively educating and leading young people through the medium of sport. Your passion for helping poverty-stricken children around the world receive adequate food and a good education may not feel fulfilled within your role as an accountant. However, distributing a portion of the income you collect from this job to donate towards an organisation committed to helping young people in impoverished circumstances can make a dramatic difference to their lives, one that couldn't have been made without your very financial support. These of course are actions that require sacrifice of either our time or resources. However, as per the earlier example of choosing to engage in a bout of exercise as opposed to remaining on the couch, these are actions that in the long run will see us having made a bigger contribution to the world around us than we otherwise would have, and will likely lead us into feeling a greater sense of personal fulfilment in the process. It should be stated here that there are circumstances when taking such actions may be beyond your current capacity or means, perhaps due to challenges related to your health, family situation, finances or otherwise. If you find yourself in such a position, then you may of course very justly feel such objectives are beyond your reach at the present time. In such cases, your energies should be committed to overcoming the circumstances you are facing and seeking out the appropriate support you may require—so that you can get back to being the friend, sibling, parent, teacher, coach, nurse or whatever other role people in your community count on you to play. In such circumstances, perhaps it is overcoming this present hardship you are facing that will allow you to live with a greater sense of meaning into the future. As previously stated, people often find a sense of meaning through enduring challenging times, through the way in which it may later enable them to help others facing similar hardships.

Whatever your situation may be, how you choose to frame your sense of life meaning will have a significant bearing on every other facet of your life, including your behaviours, your relationships and your psychological health. When it comes to our life's mission and where we choose to devote our time and energy, we are faced with a defining choice. We could frame our aspirations and sense of life purpose in an individualistic fashion, orienting our lives purely around pursuing our personal wants and desires. These could be desires that are centred on money, achieving greater levels of comfort or elevating our own level of status. Or we can utilise these many advantages modern society offers us, inclusive of the enhanced educational, financial and social liberties we are graced with, to truly pursue a life of purpose that goes beyond ourselves and, in doing so, improves the lives of those around us. This is not to put aside any aspirations we may have for living in a larger house, obtaining a job promotion, or even owning our dream car. These may be important goals for you to aspire to, and in fact, even these seemingly self-centred desires can be a part of your greater purpose, whatever you may see that purpose to be. For example, I know of a man who had done very well in business and upon his retirement decided to engage with his passion for sailing by purchasing an impressive new catamaran. This may sound like an incredibly decadent purchase, and for most of us something completely out of reach. But as this man lived out his dream of traversing the crystal blue waters of the Mediterranean Sea, the Pacific Ocean and the islands of the Caribbean, he chose to do so not just in the company of close family and friends. He used this amazing resource to invite a range of different people on board to enjoy these experiences with him. These people included his house cleaner, his neighbors, as well as yours truly. Whether he knew it or not, he was using the resources he had, as well as his passion for sailing, to gift people an experience they otherwise likely never would have had. Needless to say, most of us are not in a position to be able to purchase a sailing yacht. In contrast to this story, I know of many others who lack the necessary resources to aid anyone else financially yet are active in offering their resources of time to help out with a range of community endeavours by volunteering at local sporting clubs, youth organisations and soup kitchens. These distinct examples show us that wherever you find yourself right now, there are needs of others you can meet both now and in the future with the resources, skills, and interests you possess, no matter how great or small.

Victor Frankl penned in his famous work *Mans Search for Meaning* that: 'what man actually needs is not a tensionless state but rather the striving and struggling for some goal worthy of him'.[13] He continues to state that: 'What he needs is not the discharge of tension at any cost, but the call of a potential meaning waiting to be fulfilled'. It is difficult to imagine that by this 'potential meaning waiting to be fulfilled', he meant that we should strive to own a top-of-the-range European car or to increase our social media followership. These may be reasonable aspirations, but on their own, they should not be confused with the idea of pursuing a life of purpose. I doubt the strength of desire to achieve these ends would be significant enough to equip you with the necessary strength to endure the atrocities experienced inside a Nazi Concentration Camp as Frankl's sense of purpose did. However, your passion for, say, using your financial provisions to aid the lives of impoverished young people, diligently caring for your family, educating the next generation, or inspiring people to live healthier lives just might. These are all objectives that extend outside of ourselves and represent a more selfless and collectivistic approach to the life we are living, as well as our major aspirations for it.

A sense of meaning in life may seem distinctly removed from psychological wellbeing. However, research shows that it is intrinsically connected to achieving optimal psychological health. As psychologists Carol Ryff and Burton Singer note: 'Purpose in life and personal growth are not contributors to, but in fact defining features of positive mental health'.[14] They add that meaning, and in turn wellbeing, comes from pursuing something 'greater than yourself', and that without a sense of meaning, humans cannot truly flourish. As Friedrich Nietzsche once wrote, 'He who has a why to live can bear almost any how'. A 'why' or a purpose is also shown to provide us with greater resilience, optimism, positive affect and ultimately, wellbeing.[15] Pursuing a life of deep-seated purpose and inner meaning can help us move beyond the superficial and self-centred desires that can drive our lives in the modern world, and instead equip us to think beyond and outside of ourselves. The results of this? A deep sense of psychological nourishment and fulfilment, irrespective of circumstance.

****

Without a well-established sense of meaning in our lives, we as humans flounder. This looks very different in different social contexts, but the outcome remains the same. Reflecting, for instance, on my experiences of visiting Moynoq and the stories I heard whilst there, many people found themselves living in a context removed from their livelihoods and without adequate support in place, were left unemployed, impoverished and without hope. This, tragically, is a reality that plays out in people's lives all around the world. It may not of course be an environmental catastrophe that triggers such an outcome; it may be the breakdown of a relationship, the loss of a job, or a series of misguided decisions. Despite being far less obvious or visible, it is equally sad when one goes through life in a resource-rich environment without fully engaging oneself towards a sense of life meaning. We may for instance look to have a sense of meaning and purpose in our lives, but if it is solely focussed on fulfilling our own comforts and gains, the science tells us we will be left feeling unsatisfied. Establishing a sense of meaning and purpose that extends beyond oneself, helps others, and takes you out of your comfort zone, can guide your thinking and behaviors to go beyond focusing on your own needs and instead prioritise the needs of others. It will help direct you away from the empty promises of acquiring more material items and essentially meaningless titles, as well as overvaluing happiness and comfort, and in turn, equip you to foster a true sense of 'wellbeing'.

Chapter 10

Concluding Thoughts

Revisiting the story of my friend who I touched on at the beginning of this book, he is today, over a decade on from the time we had that initial conversation about his dealings with depression, thankfully, faring much better with his mental health. He now works a great job whereby he draws on his artistic talents to make a difference in the world and is married to the love of his life who he lives with along with their beautiful daughter. This is not a completely happily ever after tale (yet), as he does still experience periods of feeling emotionally down, crediting infrequent episodes of inner restlessness and self-doubt as the largest contributor to this psychological unease. Despite these occasional flare-ups however, the progress he has made in relation to his mental health over the past few years is significant. And, whilst he admits to having had substantial help from professional counsellors and psychologists along the way, he attributes basic lifestyle shifts as the most poignant factor in fostering this improvement.

Having initially engaged in a range of 'Westernised' antidotes aimed at alleviating his adverse symptoms, including at different times self-medicating with recreational drugs, extended trips to South America and self-confessed attempts at pursuing fame and fortune, he found out the hard way that such remedies were not providing the aid his complex condition craved. Instead, he points to having a strong and extended community of people around him, as well as a shift in his perspective around what he considered to be the most important aspects of his life that came about after marrying his now wife, as significant changes that helped alleviate his symptoms. This alteration in perspective included a calming of his self-confessed 'hyper ambitious' nature, leading him to leave his job at a big consultancy firm and instead build a career around what he was truly passionate about — teaching. It also encouraged him to grow the community of support he had around him, which now extends to a broad and diverse range of people. Indeed, this friend is now active in a number of community groups, charities as well as hobby clubs, allowing him to support and be supported by a range of other people outside his immediate circle of friends.

It would not be fair to say that all of my friend's psychological ill-health stemmed simply and exclusively from the influence of the cultural factors that have been discussed throughout this book. It is well established that biological, cognitive, personality, and circumstantial factors are all relevant in contributing to psychological health outcomes. However, the narrative my friend shared from the very beginning pointed towards issues symptomatic of the influences of modern life we have explored in the previous chapters as being, at least in part, contributors to his mental health battles. These included symptoms of feeling isolated and disconnected from the society that surrounded him, of feeling inadequate, and of chasing goals that inevitably left him feeling unfulfilled. The research we have reviewed throughout the previous chapters also pinpoints factors such as these as being highly influential over modern society's growing state of psychological unease. The improvements in my friend's psychological health over the years that coincided with him making significant lifestyle changes towards 'counter' values to those of modern society, are further suggestive that the influences of modern life were playing some sort of role in his psychological sufferings. In accordance with the earlier reviewed research findings, it seems that broadening his understanding of what makes up a 'well being', as well as implementing more 'collectivistic' and 'intrinsically' focused behaviours, have made a significant positive difference in his life.

Why was it that this friend, as well as the others I mentioned in the introduction chapter of this book, came to me detailing their mental health issues? It is likely because I went to them first. From a young age, I myself struggled with severe bouts of depression and anxiety. I'd like to say I applied the lessons and insights from this book, and I'm now entirely cured of such feelings. That would, however, be untrue for a number of reasons. Firstly, my story, much like that of the friends I have just described, has involved at times falling into the trap of focusing too much on my own needs and goals ahead of those of the community around me, to chasing material successes, as well as just 'going through the motions' and neglecting to look after the broader aspects of my wellbeing such as my social and emotional health. In addition to this, I wrote earlier that my father left behind my mum, younger brother and me when I was just five years old. This came with a significant cost to us all, and not just from the perspective of what it meant for our family dynamic. For me personally, it was my sense of self-worth and identity that suffered the most. I acknowledge that I have had many advantages and privileges afforded to me in my life. To date, my body has been relatively healthy, I have never gone without food or shelter, and the country I have lived in for most of my life is about as safe a country one can live within amidst the twenty-first century. I have visited plenty of places around the world where such comforts and security are not so easy to come by. However, dwelling on this good fortune compared to the lesser fortunes of others is a practice that is inadequate in freeing me from the feelings of abandonment, self-worth and subsequent sadness that can take root in my mind from time to time. Whilst such reflections can provide one with an immediate shift in their perspective and, in turn, lead them towards a greater level of gratitude and contentment specific to their current circumstances, it is unlikely to counter the many complex neurological, physical, and social manifestations brought about by symptoms of anxiety and depression. Yet for me, the recognition that firstly, my healing is not going to come about through the means of ticking off that next goal, obtaining greater popularity, or ignoring the adverse feelings I am experiencing and instead pursuing 'on-demand' happiness has been a significant step in helping me on towards achieving better mental health outcomes. Secondly, by actively engaging in some of the principles outlined within the previous chapters, such as being more intentionally engaged with the community that surrounds me, by letting go of external concerns such as what others may think of me, and instead appreciating the triviality of such worries in the context of human history and my very brief place in it, and by pursuing a life of meaning over one of comfort and in the moment happiness, I've gained practical coping tools for when such psychological storms have hit. As well as a series of protective buffers from how severe these storms can be.

These ideas have been the premise of this entire book, with the results of the research reviewed throughout it pointing to modern cultural values as playing an influential role in the increase of mental health issues experienced by people living in developed contexts. As we have seen, the resultant attitudes and behaviours these cultural influences can foster have become deeply embedded into our social fabric. The pursuit of individual autonomy, personal wealth and status, as well as greater happiness, has become very much normalised across our society today and, in turn, become vastly influential in framing the belief systems that govern our lives. And yet, as the psychological literature has shown us, these cultural factors are also too often overlooked in terms of how they relate to our psychological health. Somewhat paradoxically, these values and behaviours have been largely born out of dramatic improvements to human living conditions and have especially prospered in contexts that possess living standards unparalleled by any other time in history. As highlighted in the previous chapters, people across the developed world today enjoy better access to education, medical care and economic resources than ever before, which has culminated in more freedoms and opportunities to pursue the aspirations and lifestyle they desire. And yet, coinciding with these immense progresses in human living, pathological symptoms of stress, anxiety, and depression are daily realities for millions of people in environments that possess unprecedented resources necessary to achieve good psychological health and quality of life.

As a testament to these improvements, in the introduction section of this book, it was mentioned that people today living in developed and politically stable nations were significantly less likely to die from acts of physical violence than their ancestors were. Focusing on the United States, in the year 2018, a total of 15,512 deaths occurred to US citizens from acts of violence or armed combat. In the same year, this figure is damningly outnumbered by the number of deaths by suicide in the US, which totalled 48,344. In the face of the various military conflicts taking place across the globe involving the US, as well as the frequently reported acts of homicide happening within its own borders, people were more than three times as likely to take their own lives than be harmed by acts of violence. These figures are matched in other high-income countries, including for example, the UK (787 people deaths by acts of violence or combat, versus 6,507 of suicide), Germany (788 deaths by violence or combat, 3126 deaths by suicide), and Sweden (306 deaths by violence and 1455 by suicide).[1]

In his classic late nineteenth-century writings on suicide, Sociologist Emile Durkheim outlines a number of broad social rationales that can lead to suicide tendencies. Specifically, he outlines the conception of 'egoistic' suicide.[2] Durkheim describes egoistic suicide as occurring when one feels a sense of detachment and a lack of belongingness to their surrounding community. This detachment, he writes, can subsequently result in feelings of loneliness, isolation and even purposelessness, whereby this societal disconnect leads a person to feel a lack of greater meaning and direction for their lives. Tragically, these theoretical projections seem likely to be applicable to the horribly high suicide figures existent in developed countries today. Countries that otherwise allow people a level of safety that is unmatched across human history.

For decades now, modern culture, along with the associated freedoms and prosperities it fosters, has cultivated lifestyles of heightened self-sufficiency, of materialistic and hedonistic pursuits, all the while leading people to become decreasingly interested in questioning what makes for a flourishing life. These are all features of modern life shown by the research reviewed throughout this book to be contributing to the increasing instances of depression across these environments. Whilst awareness around the worsening state of society's mental health has increased exponentially in recent years, better recognising the effect our culture — along with the values and cognitions it perpetuates — is having on this decline, has been largely overlooked. As we better acknowledge how modern cultural environments can manifest as behaviours and thinking patterns that can be detrimental to our wellbeing, we can begin to be more discerning towards what is truly most important for a good life. In doing so we can shift our thinking towards values and behaviours that for millennia have allowed people to endure, and even find joy in, social contexts that harboured severe disadvantages to those in which we live today. Today, Western cultural environments encourage us to seek happiness at all costs and to do so all by ourselves. They tell us to strive for greater material wealth and gain and to prioritise these aims above all else, even our health. The research clearly condemns this approach. Instead, it points to the importance of the behaviours and cognitions these pursuits often get in the way of, such as building strong social networks, pursuing intrinsic goals, and allowing room for pain and growth in our lives, which are essential contributors to psychological health.

To conclude, I would like to elaborate on the words of Leo Tolstoy that reside on the opening page of this book. Sourced from what is considered to be one of Tolstoy's finest works of short story fiction, *The Death of Ivan Ilyich* tells the tale of Ivan Ilyich, a magistrate who lives a life that is 'most simple and most ordinary, and therefore most terrible'.[3] Ilyich is portrayed as a man intent on advancing his social standing in society, prioritising his work at the expense of his relationships with his wife and children. As the story progresses, Ilyich sustains a seemingly trivial injury, that as time goes on leads him to experience significant pain. Upon seeking medical help, Ilyich is provided with the abrupt and shocking diagnosis that his condition is so severe that he in fact has just weeks to live, and his advancing pain confining him to spend the remainder of his days bedridden. It is in this place of vulnerability and forced state of stillness that Ilyich reflects on the relentless pursuit of wealth and status he had dedicated his life towards, as well as the consequent neglect he has shown towards his wife and children, along with the things that truly matter. It is from this deliberation that we get the quote:

> It occurred to him that his scarcely perceptible attempts to struggle against what was considered good by the most highly placed people, those scarcely noticeable impulses which he had immediately suppressed, might have been the real thing, and all the rest false. And his professional duties and the whole arrangement of his life and of his family, and all his social and official interests, might all have been false.

This is a confronting, evocative, and in many ways tragic musing. It summarises the tyranny of a life revolved around materialistic pursuits, the frailties of life, and the reality of death. More than anything, it details the consequences of living a life of misguided meaning. That is, a life that lacks a true and abiding connection to what matters most. Tolstoy wrote this story well over a century ago. However, the messages embodied in its narrative seem to be more relevant today than ever before. The unfortunate reality is, much like the fate handed down to Ivan Ilyich, we are all sooner or later also going to be confronted with our own mortality. Thinking backwards from that day, we have a choice. We can continue to strive towards the 'falsities' that modern life endlessly promotes to us, such as climbing our own social ladder and living for our own self-centred pursuits. Alternatively, we can aspire to live a life that engages with, and consequently betters, the community around us. We can work towards a life of developing prosperous relationships with others, cultivating inner peace, being 'holistically' well, and ultimately a life of striving towards a purpose that transcends ourselves. Whilst such a focus won't see us immune from the many stressors and anxieties modern life cultivates, directing our life towards these means will see us best placed to optimise our psychological health amidst this environment, while also using the abundant resources and freedoms we have available to us today to buffer against the things that can detract from it.

Endnotes

Chapter 1

1 Van Zanden, J. L., Baten, J., Mira d'Ercole, M., Rijpma, A., Smith, C., & Timmer, M. (2014). *How was life? Global well-being since 1820*. Paris, France: OECD Publishing.

2 OECD. (2020). Executive summary. In *How's Life? 2020: Measuring well-being*. OECD Publishing.

3 U.S. Department of Commerce, Census Bureau. (2023). *Current Population Survey (CPS), Annual Social and Economic Supplement, 2022*.

4 Australian Institute of Health and Welfare. (2024). *Australia's health 2024: In brief* (Catalogue No. AUS 249). Australian Government.

5 OECD (2020), 'Executive summary', in: *How's Life? 2020: Measuring Well-being*, OECD Publishing, Paris.

6 Eckersley, R. (2011). A new narrative of young people's health and wellbeing. *Journal of Youth Studies, 14*(5), 627-638.

7 See for example: Twenge, J. M., Cooper, A. B., Joiner, T. E., Duffy, M. E., & Binau, S. (2019). Age, period, and cohort trends in mood disorder indicators and suicide-related outcomes in a nationally representative dataset, 2005–2017. *Journal of Abnormal Psychology, 128*, 185–199; Whiteford, H. A.,

Degenhardt, L., Rehm, J. T., Baxter, A. J., Ferrari, A. J., Erskine, H. E., ... & Vos, T. (2013). Global burden of disease attributable to mental and substance use disorders: Findings from the Global Burden of Disease Study 2010. *The Lancet, 382*, 1575–1586; and: Rutter, M., & Smith, D. J. (1995). *Psychosocial disorders in young people: Time trends and their causes.* California, CA: Wiley.

8 Haslam, N. (2016). Concept creep: Psychology's expanding concepts of harm and pathology. *Psychological Inquiry, 27*(1), 1–17.

9 Horwitz, A. V. (2010). How an age of anxiety became an age of depression. *The Milbank Quarterly, 88*(1), 112–138.

10 See for example: Twenge, J. M., Cooper, A. B., Joiner, T. E., Duffy, M. E., & Binau, S. (2019). Age, period, and cohort trends in mood disorder indicators and suicide-related outcomes in a nationally representative dataset, 2005–2017. *Journal of Abnormal Psychology, 128*, 185–199; Collishaw, S., Maughan, B., Natarajan, L., & Pickles, A. (2010). Trends in adolescent emotional problems in England: A comparison of two national cohorts twenty years apart. *Journal of Child Psychology and Psychiatry, 51*(8), 885–894; and Tick, N. T., Van der Ende, J., & Verhulst, F. C. (2008). Ten-year trends in self-reported emotional and behavioural problems of Dutch adolescents. *Social Psychiatry and Psychiatric Epidemiology, 43*(5), 349–355.

11 World Health Organization. (2017). *Depression and other common mental disorders: Global health estimates.* World Health Organization.

12 World Health Organization. (2017). *Depression and other common mental disorders: Global health estimates.* World Health Organization.

13 Twenge, J. M., Gentile, B., DeWall, C. N., Ma, D. S., Lacefield, K., & Schurtz, D. R. (2010). Birth cohort increases in psychopathology among young Americans: A cross-temporal meta-analysis of the MMPI. *Clinical Psychology Review, 30*(2),145–154.

14 Twenge, J. M., Campbell, W. K., & Freeman, E. C. (2012). Generational differences in young adults' life goals, concern for others, and civic orientation, 1966-2009. *Journal of Personality and Social Psychology, 102*, 1045–1062; Twenge, J. M., & Kasser, T. (2013). Generational changes in materialism and work centrality, 1976–2007: Associations with temporal changes in societal insecurity and materialistic role modelling. *Personality and Social Psychology Bulletin, 39*, 883–897.

Chapter 2

1 Cook, J. (1999). *The journals of Captain Cook* (P. Edwards, Ed.). Penguin Classics.

2 Kawainui Kane, H. (1997). Ancient Hawaii. Hi: Kawainui Press, p.28.

3   Eagleton, T. (2016). *Culture.* Yale University Press.

4   Diener, E. (2009). *Culture and Well-Being: The Collected Works of Ed Diener.* New York: Springer.

5   See: Twenge, J. M., Spitzberg, B. H., & Campbell, W. K. (2019). Less in-person social interaction with peers among U.S. adolescents in the 21st century and links to loneliness. *Journal of Social and Personal Relationships, 36*(6), 1892–1913; and Taylor, H. O., Cudjoe, T. K., Bu, F., & Lim, M. (2023). The state of loneliness and social isolation research: Current knowledge and future directions. *BMC Public Health, 23,* 1049.

6   Eckersley, R. (2005). *Well & Good: Morality, Meaning and Happiness (2nd Ed.).* Melbourne: Text Publishing.

7   Ryan, R. M., & Deci, E. L. (2000). Self-determination theory and the facilitation of intrinsic motivation, social development, and well-being. *American Psychologist, 55*(1), 68–78.

8   Bauman, Z. (2000). *The art of life.* Cambridge: Polity Press, p.4.

9   Clarke, A., Frijters, P., Krekel, C., & Layard, R. (2019). A happy choice: Wellbeing as the goal of government. *Behavioural Public Policy,* 1-40.

10 Bauman, Z. (2000). *The art of life.* Cambridge: Polity Press.

11 Newfield, J. (1988). *Robert Kennedy: A Memoir* (reprint ed.). Penguin Group. pp. 234–235.

12 Eckersley, R. (1998). Perspectives on progress: Economic growth, quality of life and ecological sustainability. In R. Eckersley (Ed.), *Measuring progress: Is life getting better?* (pp. 3–34). Melbourne: CSIRO Publishing.

13 Humphrey, A., Forbes-Mewett, H., & Bliuc, A.-M. (2022). "I Just want to be Happy": An Exploration of the Aspirations, Values, and Psychological Wellbeing of Australian Young People. *Emerging Adulthood, 11*(3), 572-580.

14 Smith, C., Christoffersen, K., Davidson, H., & Snell, P. (2011). *Lost in translation: The dark side of emerging adulthood.* New York: Oxford University Press.

15 Taylor, C. & Kraut, R. (1997). *Plato's Republic.* Lanham: Rowman & Littlefield Publishers.

16 Fenton, J. (2010). *William Blake.* London: Faber.

Chapter 3

1   Bauman, Z. (2000). *Liquid modernity.* Cambridge: Polity Press.

2   In one of the earliest large-scale research projects looking at cultural values across nations, Hofstede analysed data collected from nearly 90,000 partici-

pants, from over 60 different countries, and then classified countries according to different dimensions of national culture. To distinguish between nations' social tendencies, Hofstede categorised countries as either individualistic or collectivistic in their social preferences. The Western countries represented in the data almost exclusively indicated very high individualistic social tendencies and practices. See: Hofstede, G. (1980). *Cultures Consequences: International Differences in Work Related Values.* California: Sage Publications.

3   Hofstede, G., Hofstede, J., & Minkov, M. (2010). *Cultures and Organizations: Software of the Mind, Revised and Expanded 3rd Edition.* New York: McGraw-Hill USA.

4   Diener, E., Diener, M., & Diener, C. (1995). Factors predicting the subjective wellbeing of nations. *Journal of Personality and Social Psychology, 69,* 851–864.

5   Eckersley R., & Dear, K. (2002). Cultural correlates of youth suicide, *Social Science & Medicine.* 55(11), 1891-1904.

6   Durkheim, E. (1897). *Suicide: a study in sociology.* New York: The Free Press.

7   Triandis, H. (1995). *Individualism and Collectivism.* Colorado: Westview Press.

8   Humphrey, A., Bliuc, A.-M., & Molenberghs, P. (2020). The social contract revisited: A re-examination of the influence individualistic and collectivistic value systems have on the psychological wellbeing of young people. *Journal of Youth Studies, 23*(2), 160-169; Nezlek, J., & Humphrey, A. (2023). Individualism, collectivism, and well-being among a sample of emerging adults in the United States. *Emerging Adulthood, 11*(2), 520-524.

9   Triandis, H. (1995). *Individualism and Collectivism.* Colorado: Westview Press.

10 De Tocqueville, A. (2000). *Democracy in America.* Chicago: The University of Chicago

11 Putnam, R. (2000). *Bowling Alone: The Collapse and Revival of American Community.* New York: Simon & Schuster. (p. 183).

12 Putnam, R. (2000). *Bowling Alone: The Collapse and Revival of American Community.* New York: Simon & Schuster. (p. 403).

13 Cacioppo, J. T., & Cacioppo, S. (2014). Social Relationships and Health: The Toxic Effects of Perceived Social Isolation. *Social and personality psychology compass, 8*(2), 58–72.

14 Cole, S. W., Capitanio, J. P., Chun, K., Arevalo, J. M., Ma, J., & Cacioppo, J. T. (2015). Myeloid differentiation architecture of leukocyte transcriptome dynamics in perceived social isolation. *Proceedings of the National Academy of Sciences of the United States of America, 112*(49), 15142–15147.

15 Donne, J. (2012) *Donne: Selected Poetry*. London: Penguin.

16 Ahuvia, A. (2002). Individualism/collectivism and cultures of happiness: A theoretical conjecture on the relationship between consumption, culture and subjective wellbeing at the national level. *Journal of Happiness Studies, 3*, 23–36.

17 Elliot, A., & Lemert, C. (2006). *The new individualism*. London: Routledge (p.3).

18 Pope, A. (1734) *An essay on man*. London: Penguin.

19 Whipman, R. (2017). *America the Anxious*. New York: St Martins Press.

20 Aristotle. (1996). *The Nicomachean Ethics*. London: Wordsworth Editions.

Chapter 4

1 Vos, T. P., & Li, Y. (2024). The Ad Agency and Ad Content in the 1840s. *Journalism History*. 1–24.

2 Ewen, S. (2001). *Captains of Consciousness: Advertising and the Social Roots of the Consumer Culture*. New York: Basic Books.

3 See for example: Kasser, T. (2002). *The High Price of Materialism*. Cambridge: MIT Press.

4 Easterlin, R. A. (1974). Does economic growth improve the human lot? Some empirical evidence. In P. A. David & M. W. Reder (Eds.), *Nations and households in economic growth: Essays in honor of Moses Abramovitz* (pp. 89–125). New York: Academic Press.

5 See for example: Dittmar, H., Bond, R., Hurst, M., & Kasser, T. (2014). The relationship between materialism and personal well-being: A meta-analysis. *Journal of Personality and Social Psychology. 107*(5), 879–924.

6 Richins, L., & Dawson, S. (1992). A consumer values orientation for materialism and its measurement: Scale development and validation. *Journal of Consumer Research, 19*(3), 303–316.

7 Kasser, T. (2002). *The High Price of Materialism*. Cambridge: MIT Press.

8 As part of this research, Kasser and his colleagues had participants engage in a number of sessions aimed at reflecting critically on their consumer habits as well as consumer culture at large. The program also facilitated discussions about the importance of being generous with one's money, as well as encouraging participants to develop 'value-based' plans for their finances. At the completion of the program, participants showed a significant decrease in their materialistic based value scores, while also subsequently reporting improvements to their mental health. See: Kasser, T., Rosenblum, K. L., Sameroff, A. J.,

Deci, E. L., Niemiec, C. P., Ryan, R. M., et al. (2014). Changes in materialism, changes in psychological well-being: Evidence from three longitudinal studies and an intervention experiment. *Motivation and Emotion, 38*(1), 1–22.

9 Vohs, K., Mead, N., & Goode, M. (2006). The psychological consequences of money. *Science, 314*(5802), 1154–1156.

10 Bauman, Z. (2000). *Liquid modernity*. Cambridge: Polity Press.

11 Dalai Lama. (2007). *The Art of Happiness*. New York: Penguin Press.

12 Epictetus. (2008). *Discourses and Selected Writings*. London: Penguin Books.

13 Dalai Lama. (2007). *The Art of Happiness*. New York: Penguin Press.

Chapter 5

1 Butler, S. (1985). *Erewhon* (New and revised ed. with an introduction by Peter Mudford.). Penguin Classics.

2 Bastian, B. (2019). *The other side of happiness*. Melbourne: Penguin Press.

3 Schooler, J. W., Ariely, D., & Loewenstein, G. (2003). The pursuit and assessment of happiness can be self-defeating. In J. C. I. Brocas (Ed.), *The psychology of economic decisions* (pp. 41–70). Oxford, UK: Oxford University Press.

4 The phenomenon of 'overexpecting' a good time on New Year's Eve is actually neatly captured in a study conducted by US Psychologists Jonathan Schooler and Dan Ariely, who explored this as a means to better understand the processes behind overvaluing happiness. Here, Schooler and Ariley conducted a survey exploring people's plans, attitudes and expectations of their New Year's Eve celebrations, with the broader aims of trying to understand how enhanced expectations for happiness can, in fact, be very problematic for one's happiness. A few days after the night had concluded, the researchers then had those same people complete a follow up survey to gauge how much they had actually enjoyed their night, and then compared these responses with the expectations they had prior to the celebration. Interestingly, results showed those who had the greatest expectation to have a good time on New Year's Eve, were significantly more likely to be let down and disappointed about how their night played out afterwards when compared with those who had lesser expectations or plans for the night. See: Schooler, J. W., Ariely, D., & Loewenstein, G. (2003). The pursuit and assessment of happiness can be self-defeating. In J. C. I. Brocas (Ed.), *The psychology of economic decisions* (pp. 41–70). Oxford, UK: Oxford University Press.

5 Schooler, J. W., Ariely, D., & Loewenstein, G. (2003). The pursuit and assessment of happiness can be self-defeating. In J. C. I. Brocas (Ed.), *The psychology of economic decisions* (pp. 41–70). Oxford, UK: Oxford University Press.

6   See for example: Mauss, I. B., Tamir, M., Anderson, C. L., & Savino, N. S. (2011). Can seeking happiness make people unhappy? Paradoxical effects of valuing happiness. *Emotion, 11*(4), 807-815; and Mauss, I. B., Savino, N. S., Anderson, C. L., Weisbuch, M., Tamir, M., & Laudenslager, M. L. (2012). The pursuit of happiness can be lonely. *Emotion, 12*(5), 908-912.

7   Weisskopf-Joelson, E. (1955). Some Comments on a Viennese School of Psychiatry. *The Journal of Abnormal and Social Psychology. 701-703.*

8   Bastian, B., Kuppens, P., Hornsey, M. J., Park, J., Koval, P., & Yukiko, U. (2012). Feeling bad about being sad: The role of social expectancies in amplifying negative mood. *Emotion, 12(1),* 69-80. See also: Bastian, B. (2019). *The other side of happiness*, Melbourne: Penguin Press.

9   McGuirk, L., Kuppens, P., Kingston, R., & Bastian, B. (2018). Does a culture of happiness increase rumination over failure? *Emotion, 18*(6), 755-764.

10 Harvey, P., & Emmanuel, S. (ed.). (2015). *A Companion to Buddhist Philosophy.* Sussex: John Wiley & Sons, 26–31.

11 Cabanas, E., & Illouz, E. (2019). *Manufacturing happy citizens: How the science and industry of happiness control our lives.* Wiley.

12 See: Joshanloo, M. (2013). A comparison of Western and Islamic conceptions of happiness. *Journal of Happiness Studies, 14*(6), 1857–1874; and Joshanloo, M. (2014). Eastern conceptualizations of happiness: Fundamental differences with western views. *Journal of Happiness Studies, 15*(2), 475–493.

13 Ford, B. Q., Dmitrieva, J. O., Heller, D., Chentsova-Dutton, Y., Grossmann, I., Tamir, M., ... Mauss, I. B. (2015). Culture shapes whether the pursuit of happiness predicts higher or lower well-being. *Journal of Experimental Psychology, 144*(6), 1053–1062.

14 Suh, E. M. (2000). Self, the hyphen between culture and subjective well-being. In E. Diener & E. M. Suh (Eds.), *Culture and subjective well-being* (pp. 63–86). Cambridge, MA: The MIT Press.

15 Smith, C., Christoffersen, K., Davidson, H., & Snell P. (2011). *Lost in translation: The dark side of emerging adulthood.* New York: Oxford University Press, P. 71.

16 Maslow, A. (1943). A theory of human motivation. *Psychological Review, 50,* 370-396.

17 Maslow, A. (1999). *Towards a Psychology of Being. (3rd ed.).* NY: John Wiley & Sons, p.37.

18 Catalino, L. I., Algoe, S. B., & Fredrickson, B. L. (2014). Prioritizing positivity: An effective approach to pursuing happiness? *Emotion, 14*(6), 1155.

19 Humphrey, A., Szoka, R., & Bastian, B. (2021). When the pursuit of happiness backfires: The role of negative emotion valuation. *Journal of Positive Psychology, 17*(5), 611–619.

20 Harris, R. (2007). *The Happiness Trap*. NSW: Exisle Publishing, (p. 10).

21 Frankl, V. (1992). *Man's Search for Meaning*. Boston: Beacon Press.

Chapter 6

1 Smil, V. (1999). China's great famine: 40 years later. *British Medical Journal, 319*(7225), 1619-21.

2 Dikötter, F. (2010). *Mao's Great Famine: The History of China's Most Devastating Catastrophe, 1958–62*. UK: Bloomsbury.

3 Pinker, S. (2018). *Enlightenment Now*. New York: Penguin.

4 Christopher, J.C. (1999). Situating psychological well-being: exploring the cultural roots of its theory and research. *Journal of Counselling Development. 77*, 141– 52.

5 World Health Organization (1948) *Constitution of the World Health Organization*, Geneva: World Health Organization.

6 See for example: Saracci R. (1997). The World Health Organisation needs to reconsider its definition of health. *British Medical Journal, 314*(7091), 1409–1410.

7 For a deeper elaboration on the linguistic origins and subsequent definitions of health, see: Brüssow, H. (2013). What is health? *Microbiology Biotechnology, 6*(4), 341-8.

8 Ryff, C. (1989). Happiness is everything, or is it? Explorations on the meaning of psychological well-being. *Journal of Personality and Social Psychology, 57*, 1069–1081.

9 Lomas, J. (1998). Social capital and health: Implications for social health and epidemiology. *Social Science & Medicine, 47*(8), 1181–1188.

10 Hamilton, C. & Denniss, R. (2005). *Affluenza*. NSW: Allen & Unwin.

11 Humphrey, A., Barahona, F., Bretherton, E., Singh, P. & Kern, M. (2025). Perspectives of wellbeing across four cultures: Australia, India, Chile and Russia. *Psychology International*.

12 Aristotle. (1996). *The Nicomachean Ethics*. London: Wordsworth Editions.

13 Gee, G., Dudgeon, P., Schultz, C., Hart, A., & Kelly, K. (2014). Aboriginal and Torres Strait Islander social and emotional wellbeing. In P. Dudgeon, H. Milroy, & R. Walker (Eds.), *Working together: Aboriginal and Torres Strait*

Islander mental health and wellbeing principles and practice (2nd ed., pp. 55–68). Canberra: Department of the Prime Minister and Cabinet.

14 Taylor, C., & Kraut, R. (1997). *Plato's Republic*. Lanham: Rowman & Littlefield Publishers.

15 Eckersley, R. (2005). *Well & Good: morality, meaning and happiness* (2nd Ed.). Melbourne: Text Publishing.

Chapter 7

1 Kasser, T., Ryan, R.M., Couchman, C.E., & Sheldon, K.M. (2004). Materialistic values: Their causes and consequences. In T. Kasser & A. D. Kanner (Eds.), Psychology and consumer culture: The struggle for a good life in a materialistic world (pp. 11–28). Washington, DC: American Psychological Association.

2 Kasser, T. (2002). *The High Price of Materialism*. Cambridge: MIT Press.

3 Hammond, E., & Horn, D. (1954). The relationship between human smoking habits and death rates: A follow-up study of 187,766 men. *Journal of the American Medical Association, 155*(15), 1316–1328.

4 See for example: Kasser, T., Rosenblum, K. L., Sameroff, A. J., Deci, E. L., Niemiec, C. P., Ryan, R. M., et al. (2014). Changes in materialism, changes in psychological well-being: Evidence from three longitudinal studies and an intervention experiment. *Motivation and Emotion, 38*(1), 1–22; and: Lekes, N., Hope, N.H., Gouveia, L., Koestner, R., & Philippe, F.L. (2012). Influencing value priorities and increasing well-being: the effects of reflecting on intrinsic values. *Journal of Positive Psychology, 7*(3), 249–61.

5 Shah, H., & N. Marks. (2004). *A well-being manifesto for a flourishing society*. London: New Economics Foundation.

6 As available in: Hamilton, C., & Denniss, R. (2005). *Affluenza*. NSW: Allen & Unwin.

7 Eckersley, R. (2022). Culture, progress and the future: can the West survive its own myths? *Salon*.

8 Eckersley, R. (2022). Culture, progress and the future: can the West survive its own myths? *Salon*.

9 Bauman, Z. (1997). *Postmodernity and its discontents*. Cambridge: Polity Press.

10 Bauman, Z. (2000). *The art of life*. Cambridge: Polity Press, p.4.

Chapter 8

1. Sansone, R. A., & Sansone, L. A. (2010). Gratitude and wellbeing: the benefits of appreciation. *Psychiatry, 7*(11), 18–22.

2. Emmons, R.A., & McCullough, M.E. (2003). Counting blessings versus burdens: an experimental investigation of gratitude and subjective well-being in daily life. *Journal of Personality and Social Psychology, 84*(2), 377–389.

3. See for example: Wood, A. M., Froh, J. J., & Geraghty, A. W. (2010). Gratitude and well-being: A review and theoretical integration. *Clinical Psychology Review, 30,* 890–905.

4. Seligman, M. (2006). *Learned optimism: How to change your mind and your life*. USA: Vintage.

5. U.S. Census Bureau. (2021). *2021 poverty guidelines.* U.S. Department of Health and Human Services, Office of the Assistant Secretary for Planning and Evaluation.

6. Rawls, J. (1999). *A theory of justice* (Revised ed.). Cambridge, MA: Harvard University Press.

7. American Psychological Association (2015). *Stress in America: Paying with our health*. Washington DC: American Psychological Association.

8. Australian Psychological Society (2015). *Stress and wellbeing in Australia survey.* Melbourne: Australian Psychological Society.

9. World Bank. (2021). *World Development Research Group, September 2021 Report.* Geneva: World Bank.

10. WHO (2017). *Progress on drinking water, sanitation and hygiene: 2017 update and SDG baselines.* Geneva: World Health Organization (WHO) and the United Nations Children's Fund (UNICEF).

Chapter 9

1. For a masterful commentary on this, see: Baumeister, R. F. (1991). *Meanings of Life.* New York: Guilford.

2. Steger, M. F. (2009). Meaning in life. In S. J. Lopez (Ed.), *Oxford handbook of positive psychology* (2nd ed., pp. 679–687). Oxford, UK: Oxford University Press.

3. See: Steger, M. F., & Shin, J. Y. (2010). The relevance of the Meaning in Life Questionnaire to therapeutic practice: A look at the initial evidence. *The International Forum for Logotherapy, 33*(2), 95–104; Zika, S., & Chamberlain,

K. (1992). On the relation between meaning in life and psychological well-being. *British Journal of Psychology, 83*(1), 133–145; and: Brassai, L., Piko, B. F., & Steger, M. F. (2011). Meaning in Life: Is it a Protective Factor for Adolescents' Psychological Health? *International Journal of Behavioral Medicine, 18*(1), 44–51.

4 Steger, M. F. (2012). Experiencing meaning in life: Optimal functioning at the nexus of spirituality, psychopathology, and well-being. In Wong, P. T. P. (Ed.), *The human quest for meaning* (2nd ed.) (pp. 165–184). New York, NY: Routledge.

5 Frankl, V. (2004). *The doctor and the soul: From psychotherapy to logotherapy.* London, England: Souvenir.

6 Ostafin, B., & Proulx, T. (2020). Meaning in life and resilience to stressors. *Anxiety, Stress & Coping, 33*(6), 603–622.

7 Humphrey, A. & Vari, O. (2021). Meaning Matters: The impact of Self-Perceived Meaning in Life and its predictors on Psychological Stressors associated with the COVID-19 Pandemic. *Behavioural Sciences, 11*(4), 50.

8 Oishi, S. & Diener, E. (2014). Residents of Poor Nations Have a Greater Sense of Meaning in Life Than Residents of Wealthy Nations. *Psychological Science, 25*(2), 422-423.

9 See: Baumeister, R., Vohs, K., Aaker, J., & Garbinsky, E. (2013). Some key differences between a happy life and a meaningful life. *Journal of Positive Psychology, 8*(6), 505–516; Oishi, S., Choi, H., Koo, M., et al. (2020). Happiness, meaning, and psychological richness. *Affective Science, 1*(1), 107–115; and: Ryan, R. M., & Deci, E. L. (2001). On happiness and human potentials: A review of research on hedonic and eudaimonic well-being. *Annual Review of Psychology, 52*, 141–166.

10 See: Huta, V., & Ryan, R. M. (2010). Pursuing pleasure or virtue: The differential and overlapping well-being benefits of hedonic and eudaimonic motives. *Journal of Happiness Studies, 11*(6), 735–762; and Steger, M. F., Kashdan, T. B., & Oishi, S. (2008). Being good by doing good: Daily eudaimonic activity and well-being. *Journal of Research in Personality, 42*(1), 22–42.

11 Grouden, M. E., & Jose, P. E. (2015). Do sources of meaning differentially predict search for meaning, presence of meaning, and wellbeing? *International Journal of Wellbeing, 5*(1), 33 -52.

12 Baumeister, R., Vohs, K., Aaker, J., & Garbinsky, E. (2013). Some key differences between a happy life and a meaningful life. *Journal of Positive Psychology, 8*(6), 505–516

13 Frankl, V. (1992). *Man's Search for Meaning.* Boston: Beacon Press (p. 104).

14 Ryff, C. D., & Singer, B. (1998). The role of purpose in life and personal growth in positive human health. In P. Wong & P. Fry (Eds.), *The human quest for meaning* (pp. 213–236). Mahwah, NJ: Erlbaum.

15 Heintzelman, S., Trent, J., & King, L. (2013). Encounters with objective coherence and the experience of meaning in life. *Psychological Science, 24*(6), 991–998.

Chapter 10

1 For data on suicide, homicides as well as deaths by homicides and combat in different nations, see: World Data Atlas (https://knoema.com/atlas).

2 Durkheim, E. (1897). *Suicide: a study in sociology.* New York: The Free Press.

3 Tolstoy, L. (1960 ed.). *The Cossacks and Other Stories.* Middlesex: Penguin Classics.

Bibliography

Ahuvia, A. (2002). Individualism/collectivism and cultures of happiness: A theoretical conjecture on the relationship between consumption, culture and subjective wellbeing at the national level. *Journal of Happiness Studies, 3*, 23–36.

American Psychological Association (2015). *Stress in America: Paying with our health.* Washington DC: American Psychological Association.

Aristotle. (1996). *The Nicomachean Ethics,* London: Wordsworth Editions.

Australian Psychological Society (2015). *Stress and wellbeing in Australia survey.* Melbourne: Australian Psychological Society.

Australian Institute of Health and Welfare. (2024). *Australia's health 2024: In brief* (Catalogue No. AUS 249). Australian Government.

Bastian, B. (2017). So many in the West are depressed because their expected not to be. *The Conversation,* August, 2017.

Bastian, B. (2019). *The other side of happiness.* Melbourne: Penguin Press.

Bastian, B., Kuppens, P., Hornsey, M. J., Park, J., Koval, P., & Yukiko, U. (2012). Feeling bad about being sad: The role of social expectancies in amplifying negative mood. *Emotion, 12*(1), 69-80.

Bauman, Z. (2000). *Liquid modernity.* Cambridge: Polity Press.

Bauman, Z. (2001). *The individualised society.* Cambridge: Polity Press.

Bauman, Z. (2000). *The art of life.* Cambridge: Polity Press.

Bauman, Z. (1997). *Postmodernity and its discontents*. Cambridge: Polity Press.

Baumeister, R. F. (1991). *Meanings of Life*. New York: Guilford.

Baumeister, R., Vohs, K., Aaker, J., & Garbinsky, E. (2013). Some key differences between a happy life and a meaningful life. *Journal of Positive Psychology, 8*(6), 505–516.

Books, Z. (2009). What is health? The ability to adapt (Editorial). *The Lancet, 373*(9666), 781.

Brassai, L., Piko, B. F., & Steger, M. F. (2011). Meaning in Life: Is it a Protective Factor for Adolescents' Psychological Health? *International Journal of Behavioral Medicine, 18*(1), 44–51.

Butler, S. (1985). *Erewhon* (New and revised ed. with an introduction by Peter Mudford.). Penguin Classics.

Cabanas, E., & Illouz, E. (2019). *Manufacturing happy citizens: How the science and industry of happiness control our lives*. Wiley.

Cacioppo, J. T., & Cacioppo, S. (2014). Social relationships and health: The toxic effects of perceived social isolation. *Social and Personality Psychology Compass, 8*(2), 58–72.

Catalino, L. I., Algoe, S. B., & Fredrickson, B. L. (2014). Prioritizing positivity: An effective approach to pursuing happiness? *Emotion, 14*(6), 1155.

Christopher, J.C. (1999). Situating psychological well-being: exploring the cultural roots of its theory and research. *Journal of Counselling Development, 77*, 141–52.

Clarke, A., Frijters, P., Krekel, C., & Layard, R. (2019). A happy choice: Wellbeing as the goal of government. *Behavioural Public Policy*, 1-40.

Cole, S. W., Capitanio, J. P., Chun, K., Arevalo, J. M., Ma, J., & Cacioppo, J. T. (2015). Myeloid differentiation architecture of leukocyte transcriptome dynamics in perceived social isolation. *Proceedings of the National Academy of Sciences of the United States of America, 112*(49), 15142–15147.

Collishaw, S., Maughan, B., Natarajan, L., & Pickles, A. (2010). Trends in adolescent emotional problems in England: A comparison of two national cohorts twenty years apart. *Journal of Child Psychology and Psychiatry, 51*(8), 885–894.

Cook, J. (1999). *The journals of Captain Cook* (P. Edwards, Ed.). Penguin Classics.

Dalai Lama (2007). *The Art of Happiness*. New York: Penguin Press.

Deci, E. L., & Ryan, R. M. (2000). The "what" and "why" of goal pursuits: Human needs and the self-determination of behavior. *Psychological Inquiry, 11*(4), 227–268.

De Tocqueville, A. (2000). *Democracy in America.* Chicago: The University of Chicago.

Diener, E. (2009). *Culture and Well-Being: The Collected Works of Ed Diener.* New York: Springer.

Diener, E., Diener, M. & Diener, C. (1995). Factors predicting the subjective well-being of nations. *Journal of Personality and Social Psychology, 69*(5), 851–864.

Dikötter, F. (2010). *Mao's Great Famine: The History of China's Most Devastating Catastrophe, 1958–62.* UK: Bloomsbury.

Dittmar, H., Bond, R., Hurst, M., & Kasser, T. (2014). The relationship between materialism and personal well-being: A meta-analysis. *Journal of Personality and Social Psychology. 107*(5), 879–924.

Donne, J. (2012) *Donne: Selected Poetry*, London: Penguin.

Durkheim, E. (1897). *Suicide: a study in sociology.* New York: The Free Press.

Eagleton, T. (2016). *Culture.* Yale University Press.

Easterlin, R. A. (1974). Does economic growth improve the human lot? Some empirical evidence. In P. A. David & M. W. Reder (Eds.), *Nations and households in economic growth: Essays in honor of Moses Abramovitz* (pp. 89–125). New York: Academic Press.

Eckersley, R. (2022). Culture, progress and the future: can the West survive its own myths? *Salon.*

Eckersley, R. (2011). A new narrative of young people's health and wellbeing, *Journal of Youth Studies, 14*(5), 627-638.

Eckersley, R. (1998). Perspectives on progress: Economic growth, quality of life and ecological sustainability. In R. Eckersley (Ed.), *Measuring progress: Is life getting better?* (pp. 3–34). Melbourne: CSIRO Publishing.

Eckersley R., & Dear, K. (2002). Cultural correlates of youth suicide, *Social Science & Medicine. 55*(11), 1891-1904.

Eckersley, R. (2005). *Well & Good: Morality, Meaning and Happiness (2nd Ed.).* Melbourne: Text Publishing.

Elliot, A., & Lemert, C. (2006). *The new individualism.* London: Routledge.

Emmons, R. A., & McCullough, M. E. (2003). Counting blessings versus burdens: an experimental investigation of gratitude and subjective well-being in daily life, *Journal of Personality and Social Psychology, 84*(2), 377–389.

Epictetus (2008). *Discourses and selected writings.* London: Penguin Books.

Ewen, S. (2001). *Captains of Consciousness: Advertising and the social roots of the consumer culture.* New York: Basic Books.

Fenton, J. (2010). *William Blake.* London: Faber.

Ford, B. Q., Dmitrieva, J. O., Heller, D., Chentsova-Dutton, Y., Grossmann, I., Tamir, M., ... Mauss, I. B. (2015). Culture shapes whether the pursuit of happiness predicts higher or lower well-being. *Journal of Experimental Psychology, 144*(6), 1053–1062.

Frankl, V. (2004). *The doctor and the soul: From psychotherapy to logotherapy.* London, England: Souvenir.

Frankl, V. (1992). Man's Search for Meaning. Boston: Beacon Press.

Gee, G., Dudgeon, P., Schultz, C., Hart, A., & Kelly, K. (2014). Aboriginal and Torres Strait Islander social and emotional wellbeing. In P. Dudgeon, H. Milroy, & R. Walker (Eds.), *Working together: Aboriginal and Torres Strait Islander mental health and wellbeing principles and practice* (2nd ed., pp. 55–68). Canberra: Department of the Prime Minister and Cabinet.

Grouden, M. E., & Jose, P. E. (2015). Do sources of meaning differentially predict search for meaning, presence of meaning, and wellbeing? *International Journal of Wellbeing, 5*(1), 33 -52.

Harari, Y. N. (2015). *Sapiens: A brief history of humankind.* New York: HarperCollins Publishers.

Hamilton, C., & Denniss, R. (2005). *Affluenza.* NSW: Allen & Unwin.

Hammond, E., & Horn, D. (1954). The relationship between human smoking habits and death rates: A follow-up study of 187,766 men. *Journal of the American Medical Association, 155*(15), 1316–1328.

Harris, R. (2007). *The Happiness Trap.* NSW: Exisle Publishing.

Harvey, P. & Emmanuel, S. (ed.). (2015). *A Companion to Buddhist Philosophy.* Sussex: John Wiley & Sons.

Haslam, N. (2016). Concept creep: Psychology's expanding concepts of harm and pathology. *Psychological Inquiry, 27*(1), 1–17.

Heintzelman, S., Trent, J., & King, L. (2013). Encounters with objective coherence and the experience of meaning in life. *Psychological Science, 24*(6), 991–998.

Henderson, W. & Knight, T. (2012), Integrating the hedonic and eudaimonic perspectives to more comprehensively understand wellbeing and pathways to wellbeing. *International journal of wellbeing, 2*(3), 196-221.

Hofstede, G. (1980). *Cultures Consequences: International Differences in Work Related Values.* California: Sage Publications.

Hofstede, G., Hofstede, J., & Minkov, M. (2010). *Cultures and Organizations: Software of the Mind, Revised and Expanded 3rd Edition.* New York: McGraw-Hill USA.

Horwitz, A. V. (2010). How an age of anxiety became an age of depression. *The Milbank Quarterly, 88*(1), 112–138.

Humphrey, A., Bliuc, A.-M., & Molenberghs, P. (2020). The social contract revisited: A re-examination of the influence individualistic and collectivistic value systems have on the psychological wellbeing of young people. *Journal of Youth Studies, 23*(2), 160-169.

Humphrey, A., Barahona, F., Bretherton, E., Singh, P., & Kern, M. (2025). Perspectives of wellbeing across four cultures: Australia, India, Chile and Russia. *Psychology International.*

Humphrey, A., Forbes-Mewett, H., & Bliuc, A.-M. (2022). "I Just want to be Happy": An Exploration of the Aspirations, Values, and Psychological Wellbeing of Australian Young People. *Emerging Adulthood, 11*(3), 572-580.

Humphrey, A., Szoka, R., & Bastian, B. (2021). When the pursuit of happiness backfires: The role of negative emotion valuation. *Journal of Positive Psychology, 17*(5), 611–619.

Humphrey, A. & Vari, O. (2021) Meaning Matters: The impact of Self-Perceived Meaning in Life and its predictors on Psychological Stressors associated with the COVID-19 Pandemic. *Behavioural Sciences, 11*(4), 50.

Huta, V., & Ryan, R. M. (2010). Pursuing pleasure or virtue: The differential and overlapping well-being benefits of hedonic and eudaimonic motives. *Journal of Happiness Studies, 11*(6), 735–762.

Joshanloo, M. (2013). A comparison of Western and Islamic conceptions of happiness. *Journal of Happiness Studies, 14*(6), 1857–1874.

Joshanloo, M. (2014). Eastern conceptualizations of happiness: Fundamental differences with western views. *Journal of Happiness Studies, 15*(2), 475–493.

Kasser, T. (2002). *The High Price of Materialism.* Cambridge: MIT Press.

Kasser, T., Rosenblum, K. L., Sameroff, A. J., Deci, E. L., Niemiec, C. P., Ryan, R. M., et al. (2014). Changes in materialism, changes in psychological well-being: Evidence from three longitudinal studies and an intervention experiment. *Motivation and Emotion, 38*(1), 1–22.

Kasser, T., Ryan, R. M., Couchman, C. E., & Sheldon, K. M. (2004). Materialistic values: Their causes and consequences. In T. Kasser & A. D. Kanner (Eds.), *Psychology and consumer culture: The struggle for a good life in a materialistic world* (pp. 11–28). Washington, DC: American Psychological Association.

Kawainui Kane, H. (1997) *Ancient Hawaii.* HI: Kawainui Press.

Lekes, N., Hope, N. H., Gouveia, L., Koestner, R., & Philippe, F. L. (2012). Influencing value priorities and increasing well-being: The effects of reflecting on intrinsic values. *Journal of Positive Psychology, 7*(3), 249–261.

Lomas, J. (1998). Social capital and health: Implications for social health and epidemiology. *Social Science & Medicine, 47*(8), 1181–1188.

Maslow, A. H. (1943). A theory of human motivation. *Psychological Review, 50*(4), 370–396.

Mauss, I. B., Savino, N. S., Anderson, C. L., Weisbuch, M., Tamir, M., & Laudenslager, M. L. (2012). The pursuit of happiness can be lonely. *Emotion, 12*(5), 908–912.

Mauss, I. B., Tamir, M., Anderson, C. L., & Savino, N. S. (2011). Can seeking happiness make people unhappy? Paradoxical effects of valuing happiness. *Emotion, 11*(4), 807–815.

McGuirk, L., Kuppens, P., Kingston, R., & Bastian, B. (2018). Does a culture of happiness increase rumination over failure? *Emotion, 18*(6), 755–764.

Newfield, J. (1988). *Robert Kennedy: A memoir* (Reprint ed). Penguin Group.

Nezlek, J., & Humphrey, A. (2023). Individualism, collectivism, and well-being among a sample of emerging adults in the United States. *Emerging Adulthood, 11*(2), 520–524.

OECD. (2011). *How's life?: Measuring well-being*. OECD Publishing.

OECD. (2020). Executive summary. In *How's Life? 2020: Measuring well-being*. OECD Publishing.

Oishi, S., & Diener, E. (2014). Residents of poor nations have a greater sense of meaning in life than residents of wealthy nations. *Psychological Science, 25*(2), 422–423.

Oishi, S., Choi, H., Koo, M., et al. (2020). Happiness, meaning, and psychological richness. *Affective Science, 1*(1), 107–115.

Ostafin, B., & Proulx, T. (2020). Meaning in life and resilience to stressors. *Anxiety, Stress & Coping, 33*(6), 603–622.

Pope, A. (1734). *An essay on man*. London: Penguin.

Putnam, R. (2000). *Bowling alone: The collapse and revival of American community*. New York, NY: Simon & Schuster.

Rawls, J. (1999). *A theory of justice* (Revised ed.). Cambridge, MA: Harvard University Press.

Richins, L., & Dawson, S. (1992). A consumer values orientation for materialism and its measurement: Scale development and validation. *Journal of Consumer Research, 19*(3), 303–316.

Rutter, M., & Smith, D. J. (1995). *Psychosocial disorders in young people: Time trends and their causes*. California, CA: Wiley.

Ryan, R. M., & Deci, E. L. (2000). Self-determination theory and the facilitation of intrinsic motivation, social development, and well-being. *American Psychologist, 55*(1), 68–78.

Ryan, R. M., & Deci, E. L. (2001). On happiness and human potentials: A review of research on hedonic and eudaimonic well-being. *Annual Review of Psychology, 52,* 141–166.

Ryff, C. D. (1989). Happiness is everything, or is it? Explorations on the meaning of psychological well-being. *Journal of Personality and Social Psychology, 57*(6), 1069–1081.

Ryff, C. D., & Singer, B. (1998). The role of purpose in life and personal growth in positive human health. In P. Wong & P. Fry (Eds.), *The human quest for meaning* (pp. 213–236). Mahwah, NJ: Erlbaum.

Saracci, R. (1997). The World Health Organisation needs to reconsider its definition of health. *British Medical Journal, 314*(7091), 1409–1410.

Sansone, R. A., & Sansone, L. A. (2010). Gratitude and well-being: The benefits of appreciation. *Psychiatry, 7*(11), 18–22.

Schooler, J. W., Ariely, D., & Loewenstein, G. (2003). The pursuit and assessment of happiness can be self-defeating. In J. C. I. Brocas (Ed.), *The psychology of economic decisions* (pp. 41–70). Oxford, UK: Oxford University Press.

Seligman, M. (2006). *Learned optimism: How to change your mind and your life.* USA: Vintage.

Shah, H., & Marks, N. (2004). *A well-being manifesto for a flourishing society.* London, UK: New Economics Foundation.

Smil, V. (1999). China's great famine: 40 years later. *British Medical Journal, 319*(7225), 1619-21.

Smith, C., Christoffersen, K., Davidson, H., & Snell, P. (2011). *Lost in translation: The dark side of emerging adulthood.* New York: Oxford University Press.

Starch, D. (1927). *Advertising principles.* New York, NY: McGraw-Hill.

Steger, M. F. (2009). Meaning in life. In S. J. Lopez (Ed.), *Oxford handbook of positive psychology* (2nd ed., pp. 679–687). Oxford, UK: Oxford University Press.

Steger, M. F. (2012). Experiencing meaning in life: Optimal functioning at the nexus of spirituality, psychopathology, and well-being. In Wong, P. T. P. (Ed.), *The human quest for meaning* (2nd ed.) (pp. 165–184). New York, NY: Routledge.

Steger, M. F., Kashdan, T. B., & Oishi, S. (2008). Being good by doing good: Daily eudaimonic activity and well-being. *Journal of Research in Personality, 42*(1), 22–42.

Steger, M. F., & Shin, J. Y. (2010). The relevance of the Meaning in Life Questionnaire to therapeutic practice: A look at the initial evidence. *The International Forum for Logotherapy, 33*(2), 95–104.

Suh, E. M. (2000). Self, the hyphen between culture and subjective well-being. In E. Diener & E. M. Suh (Eds.), *Culture and subjective well-being* (pp. 63–86). Cambridge, MA: The MIT Press.

Taylor, H. O., Cudjoe, T. K., Bu, F., & Lim, M. (2023). The state of loneliness and social isolation research: Current knowledge and future directions. *BMC Public Health, 23*, 1049.

Taylor, C., & Kraut, R. (1997). *Plato's Republic*. Lanham, MD: Rowman & Littlefield Publishers.

Tick, N. T., Van der Ende, J., & Verhulst, F. C. (2008). Ten-year trends in self-reported emotional and behavioural problems of Dutch adolescents. *Social Psychiatry and Psychiatric Epidemiology, 43*(5), 349–355.

Tolstoy, L. (1960). *The Cossacks and other stories*. Middlesex, UK: Penguin Classics.

Triandis, H. C. (1995). *Individualism and collectivism*. Boulder, CO: Westview Press.

Twenge, J. M., Campbell, W. K., & Freeman, E. C. (2012). Generational differences in young adults' life goals, concern for others, and civic orientation, 1966–2009. *Journal of Personality and Social Psychology, 102*, 1045–1062.

Twenge, J. M., Cooper, A. B., Joiner, T. E., Duffy, M. E., & Binau, S. (2019). Age, period, and cohort trends in mood disorder indicators and suicide-related outcomes in a nationally representative dataset, 2005–2017. *Journal of Abnormal Psychology, 128*, 185–199.

Twenge, J. M., Gentile, B., DeWall, C. N., Ma, D. S., Lacefield, K., & Schurtz, D. R. (2010). Birth cohort increases in psychopathology among young Americans: A cross-temporal meta-analysis of the MMPI. *Clinical Psychology Review, 30*(2), 145–154.

Twenge, J. M., & Kasser, T. (2013). Generational changes in materialism and work centrality, 1976–2007: Associations with temporal changes in societal insecurity and materialistic role modelling. *Personality and Social Psychology Bulletin, 39*, 883–897.

Twenge, J. M., Spitzberg, B. H., & Campbell, W. K. (2019). Less in-person social interaction with peers among U.S. adolescents in the 21st century and links to loneliness. *Journal of Social and Personal Relationships, 36*(6), 1892–1913.

U.S. Census Bureau. (2021). *2021 poverty guidelines*. U.S. Department of Health and Human Services, Office of the Assistant Secretary for Planning and Evaluation.

U.S. Department of Commerce, Census Bureau. (2023). *Current Population Survey (CPS), Annual Social and Economic Supplement, 2022*.

Van Zanden, J. L., Baten, J., Mira d'Ercole, M., Rijpma, A., Smith, C., & Timmer, M. (2014). *How was life? Global well-being since 1820*. Paris, France: OECD Publishing.

Vohs, K., Mead, N., & Goode, M. (2006). The psychological consequences of money. *Science, 314*(5802), 1154–1156.

Weisskopf-Joelson, E. (1955). Some comments on a Viennese school of psychiatry. *The Journal of Abnormal and Social Psychology, 50*, 701–703.

Whipman, R. (2017). *America the anxious*. New York, NY: St. Martin's Press.

Whiteford, H. A., Degenhardt, L., Rehm, J. T., Baxter, A. J., Ferrari, A. J., Erskine, H. E., ... & Vos, T. (2013). Global burden of disease attributable to mental and substance use disorders: Findings from the Global Burden of Disease Study 2010. *The Lancet, 382*, 1575–1586.

Wood, A. M., Froh, J. J., & Geraghty, A. W. A. (2010). Gratitude and well-being: A review and theoretical integration. *Clinical Psychology Review, 30*, 890–905.

World Bank. (2021). *World Development Research Group, September 2021 Report*. Geneva: World Bank.

World Health Organization. (2017). *Progress on drinking water, sanitation and hygiene: 2017 update and SDG baselines*. Geneva, Switzerland: World Health Organization (WHO) and the United Nations Children's Fund (UNICEF).

World Health Organization. (2017). *Depression and other common mental disorders: Global health estimates*. World Health Organization.

World Health Organization. (1948). *Constitution of the World Health Organization*. Geneva, Switzerland: World Health Organization.

World Data Atlas. (n.d.). *Number of homicides*. Knoema. https://knoema.com/atlas/Number-of-homicides

Zika, S., & Chamberlain, K. (1992). On the relation between meaning in life and psychological well-being. *British Journal of Psychology, 83*(1), 133–145.

www.ingramcontent.com/pod-product-compliance
Lightning Source LLC
Chambersburg PA
CBHW061253230426
43665CB00026B/2919